The ICSA **Audit Committee Guide**

The ICSA
Audit Committee Guide

Timothy Copnell
Director, Audit Committee Institute

SPONSORED BY KPMG LLP (UK)

Published by ICSA Publishing Ltd
16 Park Crescent
London W1B 1AH

Typeset in 9.5 on 13 pt Sabon by Paul Barrett Book Production, Cambridge
and printed in Great Britain by TJ International, Padstow, Cornwall.
Project management by the Editmaster Co, Northampton.

British Library Cataloguing in Publication Data
A catalogue record for this book is available from the British Library

ISBN 1 86072 312 8

Contents

Foreword

Corporate governance excellence continues to be an important element of UK business. Expectations of stakeholders in the corporate governance process, including financial reporting, have never been higher, and the scrutiny by regulators and investors never more stringent. As a consequence, the role of the audit committee has rapidly increased in importance and expanded in scope. Today, audit committees are being asked to assume responsibilities well beyond their traditional duties.

Recognising that effective corporate governance is the cornerstone of shareholder protection, initiatives by regulators and stakeholders to help shape and guide corporate governance practices have confirmed the audit committee's key role in corporate governance and oversight. The Financial Reporting Council's revised Combined Code and the related guidance for audit committees (the Smith Guidance) contain recommendations designed to strengthen the effectiveness of audit committees, clarify and enhance their oversight roles, and enhance their accountability over the financial reporting process. Understanding the purpose and implications of these recommendations is critical in evaluating the challenges facing audit committees and the direction in which corporate governance is heading.

With an increased emphasis on the role of the audit committee in corporate governance, audit committees must assess what they are doing now and how they are doing it to ensure they are ready for the challenges ahead. The Audit Committee Institute (ACI) believes that the building blocks of an effective audit committee, from an effective agenda and committee structure to a keen awareness of current and emerging issues, are fundamental in fulfilling the audit committee's responsibilities. This publication identifies current and emerging issues that audit committees should be aware of, and react to, and describes audit committee practices that provide the support and structure necessary in fulfilling their terms of reference. We believe all audit committees can benefit from comparing their practices against the practices described in this publication in their effort to critique, tailor and improve their own practices.

In today's complex and evolving business environment, audit committees can contribute tremendously to a 'no surprises' environment. An audit committee that operates effectively is a key feature in a strong corporate governance culture and can bring significant benefits to a company. We hope this publication will help ensure that audit committees achieve their objectives and add value to the board of directors, the organisation and its stakeholders.

We owe our thanks to those who have supported the Audit Committee Institute since its formation in 2002. We believe this book will help audit committee members meet the challenges demanded of them by providing genuinely practical guidance. Our thanks in particular to Sarah Ray and John Glover, without whose efforts this book could not have been produced.

Michael Hughes
Chairman of Audit, KPMG Audit Plc

Timothy Copnell
Director, Audit Committee Institute, sponsored by KPMG LLP (UK)

About the Audit Committee Institute

Recognising the importance of audit committees, the Audit Committee Institute (ACI) has been created to serve audit committee members and help them to adapt to their changing role. Historically, audit committees have largely been left on their own to keep pace with rapidly changing information related to governance, audit issues, accounting, and financial reporting. Sponsored by KPMG LLP (UK), the ACI provides knowledge to audit committee members and a resource to which they can turn for information or to share knowledge.

The ACI's primary objective is to communicate with audit committee members and enhance their awareness and ability to implement effective audit committee processes.

The ACI aims to serve as a highly useful, informative resource for audit committee members in such key areas as:

- audit committee governance, technical and regulatory issues;
- sounding board for enhancing audit committees' process and policies; and
- surveys of trends and concerns.

For more information on the work of the ACI, please visit our website: www.kpmg.co.uk/kpmglaci/index.cfm.

Introduction

Shaping the audit committee agenda

The role of those responsible for corporate governance and the financial reporting process continues to face intense scrutiny by regulators, legislators, security analysts, institutional investors and the general public. Attention is being placed not only on the board of directors but also on those committees that have been delegated responsibility and accountability by the board. Audit committees are clearly viewed as a critical component of the overall corporate governance process. Accordingly, many audit committees are examining the nature and extent of their oversight roles, members' qualifications and independence, and their interaction and involvement with the audit process.

Effective audit committees are supported by fundamental 'building blocks' – an appropriate structure and foundation, reasonable and well-defined responsibilities, and an understanding of current and emerging issues. Only through carefully designed practices can an audit committee maximise its contribution to an organisation. Audit committees need to understand these building blocks and the specific practices that can be used in implementing governance activities. By comparing practices currently being performed to leading practices, audit committees can identify and select a 'set' of practices as the most effective and efficient in its particular circumstances. This publication describes such practices.

Audit committees have evolved from ad hoc committees with few defined responsibilities to what they are today: critical committees with growing responsibilities that are accountable to the board of directors, and ultimately to shareholders.

Brought to prominence in 1992 through Sir Adrian Cadbury's *Report on the Financial Aspects of Corporate Governance*, the duties of audit committees have grown with successive corporate governance reports. These culminated in the Financial Reporting Council's revised *Combined Code on Corporate Governance* and the related guidance for audit committees (the Smith Guidance) issued in 2003.

The Combined Code and the Smith Guidance are designed to assist boards in making suitable corporate governance arrangements. Smith provides best practice recommendations and guidance to assist directors serving on audit committees. Best practice requires that every board should consider in detail whether its audit committee arrangements are best suited for its particular circumstances. However, audit committee practices need to be proportionate to the task, and will vary according to the size, complexity and risk profile of the company.

Specific practices are not mandated. However, the Financial Services Authority's Listing Rules do require companies incorporated within the UK to report on how they apply the 14 corporate governance principles and 21 supporting principles included in the Combined Code; and confirm the extent of their compliance with the 48 detailed Combined Code provisions and explain the rationale behind any non-compliance. The Smith Guidance provides direction on how companies might apply and comply with the Combined Code provisions and principles relating to audit committees.

In recent years, events in the US have influenced corporate governance practices in the UK:

- The report by the US Blue Ribbon Committee on Improving the Effectiveness of Corporate Audit Committees (the 'Blue Ribbon Committee'), released in 1999, resulted in the New York Stock Exchange (NYSE), the National Association of Securities Dealers (NASDAQ) and the American Stock Exchange (AMEX) revising their listing requirements and mandating various audit committee practices. The recommendations also resulted in new regulations by the US Securities and Exchange Commission (SEC) regarding audit committee processes and reporting.

- The Sarbanes-Oxley Act of 2002 mandated sweeping corporate governance changes and new audit committee practices. As a result of the Act, the SEC issued new regulations pertaining to audit committees and the NYSE, NASDAQ and AMEX revised their listing requirements. In some cases, the NYSE requirements go beyond the SEC's requirements. A comparison of the Smith Guidance and the relevant recommendations of the SEC and NYSE is set out in Appendix 15.

From these developments, audit committees have evolved and improved and leading practices have emerged. Many audit committees in the UK are currently performing a number of these leading practices; however, others are not. All audit committees can benefit from comparing their practices against the practices described in this publication in an effort to improve their own practices. The Audit Committee Institute recognises that not all practices outlined in this publication will apply equally to all different entities.

Using this book

This book starts by looking at the role of the audit committee as set out by the revised Combined Code. The chapters that follow look at how to create an effective audit committee, and then how to run that committee. The last three chapters are devoted to the three fundamental responsibilities of audit committees: overseeing financial reporting; overseeing the process related to the company's financial risks and internal control; and overseeing internal and external audit processes.

For the convenience of readers, many of the documents contained in the appendices are reproduced on the accompanying CD so that they may easily be adapted to suit individual requirements. References to the relevant sections of the Smith Report are highlighted in individual boxed sections.

1   The role of the audit committee

As discussed in the introduction, audit committees are viewed by shareholders, regulators, legislators and the wider public as a critical component of an organisation's corporate governance process. However, confidence in the audit committee's ability to perform its role adequately has been diminished in light of the dramatic corporate failures in the United States and Europe in the recent past.

Following these events, and the resultant fall in confidence in the capital markets around the world, the UK Government established its Coordinating Group on Auditing and Accounting Issues, which was tasked with strengthening the UK's defences against corporate malfeasance of the kind seen in the US.

As part of this strategy Sir Robert Smith was asked by the Financial Reporting Council (FRC) to produce guidance for audit committees. The recommendations set out in the Smith Report were included in the revised Combined Code, together with the results of projects overseen by the Coordinating group. The Smith Guidance is set out in Appendix 18.

The following sets out the principles and provisions relating to the audit committee contained in the revised Combined Code.

Code principles

No one other than the committee chairman and members is entitled to be present at a meeting of the nomination, audit or remuneration committee, but others may attend at the invitation of the committee (Principle A.3).

The chairman should ensure that the directors continually update their skills and the knowledge and familiarity with the company required to fulfil their role both on the board and on board committees. The company should provide the necessary resources for developing and updating its directors' knowledge and capabilities (Principle A.5).

All directors should be submitted for re-election at regular intervals, subject to continued satisfactory performance. The board should ensure planned and progressive refreshing of the board (Principle A.7).

The board should establish formal and transparent arrangements for considering how they should apply the financial reporting and internal control principles and for maintaining an appropriate relationship with the company's auditors (Principle C.3).

Code provisions

The board should ensure that directors, especially non-executive directors, have access to independent professional advice at the company's expense where they judge it necessary to discharge their responsibilities as directors. Committees should be provided with sufficient resources to undertake their duties (Provision A.5.2).

All directors should have access to the advice and services of the company secretary, who is responsible to the board for ensuring that board procedures are complied with. Both the appointment and removal of the company secretary should be a matter for the board as a whole (Provision A.5.3).

The board should state in the annual report how performance evaluation of the board, its committees and its individual directors has been conducted. The non-executive directors, led by the senior independent director, should be responsible for performance evaluation of the chairman, taking into account the views of executive directors (Provision A.6.1).

The board should establish an audit committee of at least three, or in the case of smaller companies two, members, who should all be independent non-executive directors. The board should satisfy itself that at least one member of the audit committee has recent and relevant financial experience (Provision C.3.1).

The main role and responsibilities of the audit committee should be set out in written terms of reference, and should include:

- monitoring the integrity of the financial statements of the company, and any formal announcements relating to the company's financial performance, reviewing significant financial reporting judgements contained in them;
- reviewing the company's internal financial controls and, unless expressly addressed by a separate board risk committee composed of independent directors, or by the board itself, to review the company's internal control and risk management systems;
- monitoring and reviewing the effectiveness of the company's internal audit function;
- making recommendations to the board, for it to put to the shareholders for their approval in general meeting, in relation to the appointment, re-appointment and removal of the external auditor and to approve the remuneration and terms of engagement of the external auditor;
- reviewing and monitoring the external auditor's independence and objectivity and the effectiveness of the audit process, taking into consideration relevant UK professional and regulatory requirements; and
- developing and implementing policy on the engagement of the external auditor to supply non-audit services, taking into account relevant ethical guidance regarding the provision of non-audit services by the external audit firm; and to report to the board, identifying any matters in respect of which it considers

that action or improvement is needed and making recommendations as to the steps to be taken (Provision C.3.2).

The terms of reference of the audit committee, including its role and the authority delegated to it by the board, should be made available. A separate section of the annual report should describe the work of the committee in discharging those responsibilities (Provision C.3.3).

The audit committee should review arrangements by which staff of the company may, in confidence, raise concerns about possible improprieties in matters of financial reporting or other matters. The audit committee's objective should be to ensure that arrangements are in place for the proportionate and independent investigation of such matters and for appropriate follow-up action (Provision C.3.4).

The audit committee should monitor and review the effectiveness of the internal audit activities. Where there is no internal audit function, the audit committee should consider annually whether there is a need for an internal audit function and make a recommendation to the board, and the reasons for the absence of such a function should be explained in the relevant section of the annual report (Provision C.3.5).

The audit committee should have primary responsibility for making a recommendation on the appointment, reappointment and removal of the external auditors. If the board does not accept the audit committee's recommendation, it should include in the annual report, and in any papers recommending appointment or reappointment, a statement from the audit committee explaining the recommendation and should set out reasons why the board has taken a different position (Provision C.3.6).

The annual report should explain to shareholders how, if the auditor provides non-audit services, auditor objectivity and independence is safeguarded (Provision C.3.7).

Listing Rules

It should be noted that the Listing Rules of the UK Listing Authority require UK incorporated listed companies to include within their annual reports:

- a statement of how it has applied the Combined Code principles, providing sufficient explanation to enable its shareholders to evaluate properly how the principles have been applied; and
- a statement as to whether or not it has complied throughout the accounting period with the Combined Code provisions. A company that has not complied with the Code provisions, or complied with only some of the Code provisions or (in the case of provisions whose requirements are of a continuing nature) complied for only part of an accounting period, must specify the Code provisions with which it has not complied, and (where relevant) for what part of the period such non-compliance continued, and give reasons for any non-compliance.

The ethos of the revised Combined Code continues to be 'comply or explain', which affords company boards a degree of flexibility. In essence it means that where a company does not comply with the Code's provisions it is required to provide an explanation. This is in stark contrast with SEC audit committee regulations in the US, where non-compliance would lead to a de-listing. Corporate governance in the US is based on regulation rather than recommendation, and its requirements are very prescriptive. Appendix 15 compares the recommendations of the Smith Guidance for Audit Committees, to selected elements of SEC and NYSE regulations relating to audit committees.

2 Creating an effective audit committee

Audit committees are established by boards of directors to help discharge their fiduciary responsibility. How the committee fulfils that mandate varies according to the clarity of the committee's mission, the abilities of the committee's members, and the tone set at the top of the governance structure. An audit committee that operates effectively is a key feature in a strong corporate governance culture and can bring significant benefits to the company.

In this chapter we present some of the characteristics that, based on our experience at the ACI, mark a strong and effective audit committee. These characteristics should be viewed not as elements carved in stone, but as components in a process that can – and should – be continually improved to enhance the committee's effectiveness.

Membership

Audit committee composition

The Combined Code recommends that audit committees should comprise at least three independent non-executive directors (two, for companies outside the FTSE 350). However, the size of the audit committee will vary depending upon the needs and culture of the company and the extent of delegated responsibilities to the committee. The objective is to allow the committee to function efficiently, all members to participate, and an appropriate level of diversity of experience and knowledge. Committees of three to six individuals are generally most appropriate to achieve those objectives.

> Appointments should be for a period of up to three years, extendable by no more than two additional three-year periods, so long as members continue to be independent.
>
> *Smith Guidance*

Appointments to the audit committee should be made by the board on the recommendation of the nomination committee (where there is one), in consultation with the audit committee chairman. Terms of three years, with staggered expiration dates to ensure continuity, are common in business today. Many companies have no set policies for rotating committee members but depend on weighing a member's experience against the risks of complacency. Without a rotation policy, it is important for the board of directors to evaluate an audit committee member's performance to see that it meets both the board's and committee's expectations.

> All members of the committee should be independent non-executive directors. The
> chairman of the company should not be an audit committee member.
>
> *Smith Guidance*

Independence

Audit committee independence is the cornerstone of the committee's effectiveness, particularly when overseeing a company's financial reporting integrity and evaluation of areas where judgements and decisions are significant. Audit committee members must be adept at communicating with management and the auditors and ready to ask key, probing questions about the company's financial risks and accounting and financial reporting.

It is up to the board to assess the integrity and independence of an audit committee candidate, so every member's appointment is an occasion for careful deliberation. The board should have a strong understanding of the relevant definitions of independence and how a lack of independence occurs and is interpreted in practice. Independence issues are most prevalent with respect to business relations. The board should also be cognisant and mindful of situations in which the definition of independence is met; yet perceived conflicts of interest may still arise.

Independence

The Combined Code states that the board should determine whether a director is independent in character and judgement and whether there are relationships or circumstances which are likely to affect, or could appear to affect, their judgement. Such relationships and circumstances include where the director:

- has been an employee of the company or group within the last five years;
- has, or has had within the last three years, a material business relationship with the company either directly, or as a partner, shareholder, director or senior employee of a body that has such a relationship with the company;
- has received or receives additional remuneration from the company apart from a director's fee, participates in the company's share option or a performance-related pay scheme, or is a member of the company's pension scheme;
- has close family ties with any of the company's advisers, directors or senior employees;
- holds cross-directorships or has significant links with other directors through involvement in other companies or bodies;
- represents a significant shareholder; or
- has served on the board for more than nine years from the date of their first election.

Compliance with the revised Combined Code requires that audit committees should comprise at least three independent non-executive directors – two for companies outside the FTSE 350. For the avoidance of doubt, the Combined Code does not consider a board chairman to be independent in this context.

Financial expertise and other skills

All audit committee members would normally be expected to have experience of financial matters, and at least one member should have recent and relevant financial experience. It is desirable that the member with recent and relevant financial experience should have a professional qualification from one of the professional accountancy bodies.

Smith Guidance

Like any non-executive director, audit committee members should (at least as a group) possess a wide range of knowledge, skills and personal attributes: sound judgement; integrity and high ethical standards; strong interpersonal skills; and the ability and willingness to challenge and probe. Specifically, audit committee members must have expertise, or access to expertise, that goes beyond mere familiarity with financial statements. They must be able to understand the rules and, more importantly, the principles that underpin the preparation of financial statements. They must be prepared to invest the time necessary to understand why critical accounting policies are chosen and how they are applied, and satisfy themselves that the end result fairly reflects their understanding.

The Combined Code states that the board should satisfy itself that at least one member of the audit committee has recent and relevant financial experience. It is sensible that the other members are, at least, financially literate.

Recent and relevant financial experience is deliberately undefined – each board should determine its own criteria. However, it is clear that it must go beyond a basic familiarity with financial statements and perhaps comprise past employment experience, or a qualification, in finance or accounting or related service that may include experience as a CEO with financial reporting oversight responsibilities, or finance director.

Some commentators have suggested that the audit committee member with the highest level of financial expertise should also chair the committee, but this need not necessarily be the case. The member who is designated as having 'financial experience' should be aware of his role, but it is not necessary for them to be identified in the annual report and accounts. For companies which have or will raise capital in foreign jurisdictions involving additional financial reporting obligations, audit committees should consider having at least one member of the audit committee with accounting or financial management expertise in that foreign country.

Members should have experience in areas pertinent to the business. A committee's effectiveness in performing its mission is certainly enhanced by, and is often dependent upon, the members' experience, knowledge and competence in business matters, financial reporting, internal controls and auditing.

The US definition of financial expert

In determining whether the audit committee has a member with recent and relevant financial experience, the board could consider the Securities Exchange Commission's (SEC) rules relating to the definition of an audit committee financial expert – a requirement for audit committees in US listed companies. The SEC define a financial expert as a person who has *all* of the following attributes:

- an understanding of generally accepted accounting principles and financial statements;
- the ability to assess the general application of such principles in connection with the accounting for estimates, accruals and reserves;
- experience of preparing, auditing, analysing or evaluating financial statements that present a breadth and level of complexity of accounting issues that are generally comparable to the breadth and complexity of issues that can reasonably be expected to be raised by the registrant's financial statements, or experience of actively supervising one or more persons engaged in such activities;
- an understanding of internal controls and procedures for financial reporting; and
- an understanding of audit committee functions.

The SEC rules go on to set out that an individual may not be considered an audit committee financial expert solely by virtue of their prior service as an audit committee member – they must have acquired the attributes of an audit committee financial expert through:

- education or experience as a principal financial officer, principal accounting officer, controller, public accountant, or auditor, or experience in one or more positions that involve the performance of similar functions;
- experience actively supervising a principal financial officer, principal accounting officer, controller, public accountant, auditor, or person performing similar functions;
- experience overseeing or assessing the performance of companies or public accountants with respect to the preparation, auditing, or evaluation of financial statements; or
- other relevant experience.

To help understand who might qualify as a financial expert, as defined by the SEC, a US financial expert decision tree is included in Appendix 17.

Resources

Audit committee remuneration

> Each company should consider the further remuneration that should be paid to members of the audit committee to recompense them for the additional responsibilities of membership.
>
> *Smith Guidance*

Audit committee members must be adequately remunerated for their services. In many public companies, deciding on the amount of remuneration is usually the responsibility of the remuneration committee. It is reasonably well established in practice that the committee chairman receives more remuneration than other members, reflecting their greater responsibilities. Moreover, the board may acknowledge that audit committee service warrants higher compensation than other board committees, in recognition of the responsibilities and increased time commitment. Consideration should be given to the time members are required to give to audit committee business, the skills they bring to bear and the onerous duties they take on, as well as the value to the company of their work. In addition to a yearly fee, some companies may offer payment for each meeting attended.

Remuneration for service can sometimes pose a dilemma for both management and committee members. While compensation should be enough to recognise the time commitment required and the liabilities accepted in order to attract good and responsible directors, the amount should not be excessive such that a conflict may be perceived.

Audit committee resources

The audit committee should be provided with sufficient resources to undertake its duties. It should have access to the services of the company secretary on all audit committee matters including assisting the chairman in planning the audit committee's work, drawing up meeting agendas, maintenance of minutes, drafting of material about its activities for the annual report, collection and distribution of information and provision of any necessary practical support. The company secretary should ensure that the audit committee receives information and papers in a timely manner to enable full and proper consideration to be given to the issues.

The board should make funds available to the audit committee to enable it to take independent legal, accounting or other advice when the audit committee reasonably believes it necessary to do so.

Professional development

Training should be provided on an ongoing and timely basis and should include an understanding of the principles of and developments in financial reporting and related company law.

Smith Guidance

All members should seek periodic continuing professional education both inside and outside the boardroom. Management, internal and external auditors, and the company secretary are sources of background information and training for audit committee members. Periodic briefings, reports and presentations by management, external auditors and internal auditors for audit committee members should cover operational and financial issues specific to the company and the industry, and updates on new accounting and auditing standards. Companies should offer, and committees should insist on, the kind of training that can enhance their financial literacy and make it possible for them to fulfil their fiduciary responsibilities.

> The company should provide an induction programme covering the role of the audit committee, including its terms of reference and expected time commitment by members; and an overview of the company's business, financial dynamics and risks.
>
> *Smith Guidance*

This is especially true of new members, who should receive a complete orientation that allows them to function effectively from the very beginning.

3   Running an effective audit committee

This chapter looks at the practices that, based on our experience, mark a strong and effective audit committee, from the terms of reference through to monitoring the committee's performance.

Audit committee terms of reference

The main role and responsibilities of the audit committees should be set out in written terms of reference and approved by the board. The terms of reference should be made available to the public, and should set out explicitly the role and responsibilities of the audit committee with respect to its relationship and expectations of internal and external auditors, its oversight of internal control, and disclosure of financial and related information.

Smith Guidance

In essence, the focus of the audit committee terms of reference should define the scope of the committee's oversight responsibilities and how these are to be discharged. The role of the audit committee is for the board to decide and it should tailor its terms of reference to the company's specific needs and clearly outline the committee's duties and responsibilties, including structure, process and membership requirements. The terms of reference should ideally describe the background and experience requirements for committee members and set guidelines for the committee's relationship with management, the internal and external auditors, and others.

An audit committee's terms of reference and responsibilities should be coordinated with other committee responsibilities—some companies have a risk committee, others have committees focused on a particular business risk (e.g. investment committee, environmental committee, etc.). Care should be taken to define clearly the roles and responsibilities of each. Terms of reference should be detailed enough to clarify roles and responsibilities, but not so detailed that they include items that cannot be reasonably accomplished. The terms of reference should serve as a guide in establishing the audit committee work plan and meeting agendas. The work plan would specifically set out how the audit committee intends to fulfil each of its responsibilities as disclosed in the terms of reference. Terms of reference prepared by the audit committee should be approved by the board. Appendix 1 and the CD which accompanies this book include an example audit committee terms of reference to assist committees in creating or updating their complete terms of reference consistent with the Smith Guidance and leading practices.

It is very important that the audit committee takes into consideration the responsibilities laid out in the terms of reference and related work plan as each meeting's agenda is set, and that all responsibilities are reviewed on at least an annual basis. This review could be incorporated into any self-evaluation process that the audit committee undertakes.

> The audit committee should review annually its terms of reference and its own effectiveness and recommend any necessary changes to the board. The board should review the audit committee's effectiveness annually.
>
> *Smith Guidance*

Once established, the audit committee terms of reference should be updated annually. The annual assessment of the committee's terms of reference should be a robust process reflecting changes to the company's circumstances and any new regulations that may impact the audit committee's responsibilities.

The revised Combined Code recommends that the audit committee terms of reference be disclosed to shareholders through inclusion on the company's websites – most listed companies now do this. However, audit committees should be mindful of the implications of increased disclosure and should ensure they are not undertaking so many responsibilities that these cannot be reasonably accomplished, or that may subject the committee to future liability.

Audit committee meetings

A detailed agenda is vital for keeping the committee focused. Effective agendas are set with input from the CEO, finance director and the internal and external auditors. The audit committee chairman, however, should maintain accountability for the agenda and not delegate it to management. The audit committee agenda for the year should ideally originate from a detailed work plan. In turn, the detailed work plan would originate from the terms of reference. Appendix 3 and the accompanying CD include an example of audit committee agenda topics that should be considered when developing detailed audit committee agendas for the year. An example audit committee agenda for the year is presented as Appendix 2. Both documents are also included on the CD.

> It is for the audit committee chairman, in consultation with the company secretary, to decide the frequency and timing of its meetings.
>
> *Smith Guidance*

There should be as many meetings as the audit committee's role and responsibilities require. The Smith Guidance recommends that there should be no fewer than three meetings during the year, held to coincide with key dates within the financial reporting and audit cycle. However, audit committee chairmen may wish to call more frequent meetings. The ACI's review of FTSE 100 corporate governance statements issued in the 2003/4 reporting season, we found that on average companies were having four meetings a year. The key is to ensure that there is sufficient time to cover all agenda items and allow time for all parties to ask questions or provide input. There should also be adequate time for the committee members to have a private session at each meeting.

Sufficient time should be allowed to enable the audit committee to undertake as full a discussion as may be required. A sufficient interval should be allowed between audit committee meetings and main board meetings to allow any work arising from the audit committee meeting to be carried out and reported to the board as appropriate.

This is all very much common sense, but should questions of substance be raised for the first time at the final audit committee meeting? Serious problems may result if such questions are answered in a way that is different from that which might be expected. If the final audit committee meeting is to be conducted effectively, then the chairman should be entering into communication with both the finance director and internal and external auditors some time in advance of the audit committee meeting and bringing matters of concern to the attention of the audit committee members. The relationship with the auditor should be such that any serious concerns are brought to the audit committee's attention promptly, though in a non-adversarial way.

No one other than the audit committee members should be entitled to attend any meeting of the audit committee. It is the audit committee itself that should decide who should attend any particular meeting (or part of a meeting). It is to be expected that the external audit lead partner, head of internal audit and the finance director will regularly be invited to attend meetings as well as perhaps the CEO or group chairman. Others may be invited to attend. The CEO often has vital insights to share; however, the audit committee chairman should ensure that the CEO does not inhibit open discussion at the meeting.

> The audit committee should, at least annually, meet the external and internal auditors, without management, to discuss matters relating to its remit and any issues arising from the audit.
>
> *Smith Guidance*

Management should be expected to discuss key accounting estimates and subjective adjustments for each interim period. External auditors should periodically discuss the appropriateness of accounting, including accounting alternatives and choices made by management. Private executive sessions should be held with the external auditors at least once a year. Leading practice would also suggest private sessions with the head of internal audit.

Opinions differ as to when private sessions with the auditors should be held. Most often such sessions are held at the end of scheduled audit committee meetings. The executives are asked to leave and the committee then invites comments from, and asks questions of, the external auditor. However, there is an emerging practice whereby the committee meets with the external auditor before the executives are invited to attend – i.e. at the beginning of the audit committee meeting. The advantage is that the committee can be fully briefed on all the issues and therefore in a better position to both understand and challenge management.

Formal meetings of the audit committee are at the heart of its work. However, they may be insufficient. The audit committee chairman, and to a lesser extent the other members, may need to keep in touch with the board chairman, the chief executive, the finance director, the external audit lead partner and the head of internal audit on a continuing basis.

Formal minutes should be prepared, circulated to external and internal auditors as appropriate, approved by the audit committee and then reviewed by the full board of directors. Important documents related to the meeting should be attached to the minutes, including the agenda.

Communication policies

The content, timing and manner in which information is released both internally and externally by the company requires levels of accountability and approval that should be defined, documented and approved by the board. Such policies should consider guidelines to help ensure communications are not selective. Policies should also consider crisis communications and electronic communication risks and controls. While these policies should be set at board level, the audit committee should, as a minimum, actively contribute to setting the policies as they relate to communication of financial information.

Assessing audit committee effectiveness

Performance evaluation is a new requirement. The revised Combined Code states that the board should undertake a formal and rigorous annual evaluation of its own performance and that of its committees and individual directors. The ACI's review of FTSE 100 corporate governance statements issued in the 2003/4 reporting season showed that companies were either still developing systems to address this requirement, or had performed performance evaluation at board level for the first time in 2003/4.

The process adopted to assess performance needs to be thought through carefully; there is no 'one size fits all' approach. However, for any appraisal process to work effectively there are some fundamental elements that must be present:

- *Independent control and objectivity.* To be credible and accountable, board and director evaluation processes must be independent of executive influence. The chairman, supported by the independent directors, should originate and control the assessment taking into consideration the views of the CEO. The option of using external consultants to assist with the design and implementation could give the added benefit of bringing objectivity to the process.
- *Positive.* If board evaluation is to be more than a box-ticking exercise, it must be designed to encourage colleagues to be candid and constructive in their evaluation of each other's performance as individual directors as well as their collective performance as a board.
- *Tailoring evaluations to the company and the board.* Boards should establish a process, including procedures and performance criteria, that suits the individuals and the company concerned.
- *Ensuring confidentiality and trust.* Boards should encourage openness, fairness and discretion in the evaluation process while ensuring it maintains strict confidentiality with respect to each participant's input and feedback.
- *Regular review of the evaluation process.* Boards should periodically review assessment practices and criteria to measure their effectiveness and responsiveness against changing needs, and to ensure continuing efficiency and appropriateness.
- *Feedback.* To ensure credibility, it is important that those involved in the evaluation process receive constructive feedback.

> The audit committee should review annually its terms of reference and its own effectiveness and recommend any necessary changes to the board. The board should review the audit committee's effectiveness annually.
>
> *Smith Guidance*

The board should review the audit committee's effectiveness by requesting feedback on the committee's performance from senior management, and the internal and external auditors. In addition, the audit committee should assess its own effectiveness and the adequacy of its terms of reference, work plans, and forum of discussion and communication by:

- questioning the board about its satisfaction with the committee's performance;
- comparing the committee's activities to the recommendations of the Smith Guidance and the guidelines of the relevant securities exchanges;
- comparing the committee's activities to leading practices;
- comparing the committee's activities to the terms of reference and any other objectives the board set for the committee; and
- consulting with external auditors on ways to improve the audit committee's performance.

An example self-assessment checklist is shown in Appendix 4 and is included on the accompanying CD.

Each of these steps would not necessarily be performed annually, but all steps should be performed every two to three years. Any necessary changes should be recommended to the board.

The chairman of the audit committee should also assess the performance of individual committee members on an annual basis.

The result of this assessment should be a recommendation to the board as to whether the member should be appointed for an additional term. The evaluation of the chairman would be done by the board based upon similar criteria. Evaluations that are well performed demonstrate the committee's intention and commitment to achieve its responsibilities in an effective and diligent manner.

What marks a member who is successful?

Someone who is dedicated to the committee's work and responsibilities, someone who is willing to devote the time necessary to understand the company and prepare for, attend and participate in meetings and deliberations, someone with an inquiring attitude, objectivity, independence and sound judgement.

---

4 Overseeing financial reporting

Audit committee responsibilities

The principal responsibility of the audit committee is to oversee the company's financial reporting process. The Smith Report states that the audit committee should monitor the financial integrity of the financial statements and any formal announcements relating to the company's financial performance.

As part of its review, the audit committee should ensure they are made aware of accounting policy or disclosure issues and that this information is communicated to them early enough to enable appropriate action to be taken as needed. The audit committee should inquire of management and/or the auditors regarding:

- recommended audit adjustments and disclosure changes, those made by management and those not made by management;
- the accounting principles and critical accounting policies adopted by management;
- unusual transactions; and
- accounting provisions and estimates included in the financial statements. A thorough understanding of all of these factors is integral to the committee's ability to meet its oversight responsibilities.

> The audit committee should review the significant financial reporting issues and judgements made in connection with the preparation of the financial statements, interim reports, preliminary announcements and related formal statements.
>
> *Smith Guidance*

The recent publicity concerning a number of high-profile irregularities has intensified both regulators' and the investing public's interest in the propriety of a company's financial reporting. In an environment where missing analysts' expectations by a small amount can lead to significant decreases in share price, market capitalisation and overall investor confidence, this focus is hardly surprising. As a result, audit committees would be prudent to sharpen their focus on current and emerging issues and to respond accordingly. Understanding the company's financial statements is therefore crucial for audit committee members.

> Taking into account the external auditor's view, the audit committee should consider whether the company has adopted appropriate accounting policies and, where necessary, made appropriate estimates and judgements.
>
> *Smith Guidance*

In general, audit committees should assume the following responsibilities:

- to understand management's responsibilities and representations;
- to understand and assess the appropriateness of management's selection of accounting principles and the most critical accounting policies;
- to understand management's judgements and accounting estimates applied in financial reporting;
- to understand the communications received from the external auditors concerning their responsibilities under generally accepted auditing standards;
- to confer with both management and the external auditors about the statements;
- to assess whether financial statements are complete and fairly presented and that disclosures are clear and transparent; and
- to review earnings releases, financial statements, and other information presented with the financial statements, prior to release.

> The audit committee should review related information presented with the financial statements, including the operating and financial review, and corporate governance statements relating to the audit and to risk management. Similarly, where board approval is required for other statements containing financial information, whenever practicable, the audit committee should review such statements first.
>
> *Smith Guidance*

The Smith Guidance recommends that the audit committee's oversight role be extended beyond the financial statements and related information (e.g. the operating and financial review, and corporate governance statements relating to the audit and to risk management), to include, where practicable, the review of other statements containing financial information and requiring board approval (e.g. significant financial returns to regulators, release of price sensitive information and summary financial statements). Often it will not be practicable for an audit committee to review such statements before board approval. Where this is the case, the audit committee should satisfy itself that adequate control processes are in place.

It is management's, not the audit committee's nor the auditor's, responsibility to prepare complete and accurate financial statements and disclosures in accordance with financial reporting standards and applicable rules and regulations. However, the audit committee needs to assure itself that the external auditors are satisfied that the accounting estimates and judgements made by management, and management's selection of accounting principles, reflect an appropriate application of generally accepted accounting practice (GAAP). The appropriateness, including the degree to which management bias, if any, is evident, of the company's accounting principles and underlying estimates and the transparency of the financial disclosures in reflecting financial performance would be at the core of discussions between the audit committee and external auditor. The committee should be interested in discussing and understanding the auditors' views on accounting issues, and should actively seek to develop a relationship with the external auditor that allows a full, frank and timely discussion of all material issues.

Communications from external auditors

Statement of Auditing Standard 610 *Communication of audit matters to those charged with governance* requires auditors to communicate:

- expected modifications to the auditors' report;
- unadjusted misstatements;
- material weaknesses in the accounting and internal control systems identified during the audit;
- their views about qualitative aspects of the entity's accounting practices and financial reporting;
- matters specifically required by other Auditing Standards to be communicated; and
- any other relevant matters relating to the audit.

During the year, the external auditor's review of interim financial information can be a valuable resource to the audit committee as the committee fulfils its oversight responsibility for financial reporting. Further recommendations on the relationship between the audit committee and the external auditor are set out in chapter 6.

Recent developments in the financial reporting environment

It is essential that management and the audit committee remain abreast of recent developments in financial reporting and recent regulatory actions. Recent years have been marked by rapid and widespread developments in financial reporting. These developments reflect the increasingly complex and innovative nature of business transactions in today's business world, and address the growing information needs of the users of financial statements. In addition, changes in financial reporting have also been promulgated by the international harmonisation and convergence of accounting standards as a result of globalisation.

International Financial Reporting Standards

Listed groups in the European Union are required to apply International Financial Reporting Standards (IFRS) in their financial statements for accounting periods beginning on or after 1 January 2005.

While UK accounting standards share much in common with IFRS, in more complex areas, and in the detail, there remain significant differences that can lead to both increased volatility (e.g. accounting for derivatives, share options, pensions and investment properties) and step changes on conversion (e.g. accounting for development costs, convertible debt and preference shares).

Staying abreast and fully understanding the implications of developments in financial reporting has become increasingly difficult, especially for companies that engage in a wide variety of business transactions or have reporting responsibilities in both the UK and the US. For example, a company that employs stock-based compensation, engages in derivative or off-balance sheet transactions, sells products through innovative sales channels, and that has recently completed one or more business acquisitions, faces stringent and complex accounting requirements – with even more on the horizon. In addition to new accounting developments, government legislation and securities exchange regulations are expanding the reporting requirements of public companies.

Audit committees must satisfy themselves that management has devoted sufficient attention to understanding recent developments in financial reporting and that the application of new requirements is appropriate in light of the nature of the company's business and significant transactions.

What steps can the audit committee take in preparing for this challenge?

First and foremost, audit committee members must educate themselves appropriately – this is often achieved by asking management or the external auditors to describe and explain recent developments in financial reporting. Armed with this knowledge, audit committees should ask probing questions of management of how new reporting standards influence and affect the financial reporting of the company, and how any unique or unusual aspects of significant transactions are being captured and portrayed in the company's financial statements and earnings releases.

Earnings management

Another area which the audit committee must remain alert to is management's approach to earnings management. Are management reporting operations in a clear and responsible way? Could the company satisfactorily respond to a regulator's inquiry into earnings management?

Recent high-profile irregularities reported in the press have been attributed to various earnings management practices. These include questionable revenue recognition; inappropriate deferral of expenses; and misconstrued recognition, reversal, or use of reserves without events or circumstances to justify such actions. These practices have come to the attention of securities regulators and others reviewing companies' accounting policies and procedures, and have led to questions about the quality of reported earnings.

Information is the lifeblood of the capital markets. If a company fails to provide meaningful disclosure to investors about where it has been, where it is and where it is going, a damaging pattern ensues. The bond between shareholders and the company is shaken; investors grow anxious; prices fluctuate; and the trust that is the bedrock of capital markets is severely tested.

Earnings management is a problem that is perhaps more widespread than we might think. Everyone, in whatever field, who has information to impart wishes to manage the way in which the information is communicated and the particular message or 'spin' that it is to be given. Management is not immune from this temptation, and earnings management is one of the ways in which this is done.

It is important that audit committees recognise the circumstances where the pressure arises. It could be that:

- market expectations are unrealistic; or
- targets are not being met; or
- management are heavily incentivised.

The pressure to achieve earnings targets can place a heavy burden on senior management, in terms of both job security and remuneration. Unfortunately, this pressure can all too often lead to the consideration of aggressive and sometimes incorrect financial reporting interpretations.

Audit committees need to know enough about their company to recognise when these conditions are present and, in that case, they need to receive what they hear with some scepticism. If audit committees do not do this, many of the improvements in the quality and reliability of financial reporting of recent years may be undermined just when they are most needed.

Auditors also must play their part. No auditor should be unaware of the problem. The traditional audit qualities of rigour and scepticism will be needed, but they may not be enough. Even if the auditor recognises what is going on, there may be little that can be done about it, if it falls within certain bounds. The auditor's role is to express an opinion on the truth and fairness of the accounts, and these are usually tested by reference to accounting standards and other requirements having regard to materiality.

Accounting standards do not, however, produce financial statements that are 'right' in the sense that there is only one possible answer. They are not a straitjacket, but are based on principles which allow them to adapt to changing circumstances. Their application can sometimes produce a range of possible answers. For example, valuations and estimates, which inevitably require judgement, are needed in relation to many elements of the financial statements – particularly in relation to transactions that span the year-end, or several years.

The potential benefits of this inherent flexibility are that it allows accounting to keep pace with business innovations. The downside is that abuses such as earnings management can occur when people exploit this pliancy. This is why the highest standards of objectivity, integrity and judgement should be the rule, not the exception.

How should audit committee members respond?

Audit committee members must fulfil their fiduciary responsibility; they should understand the company; they should be briefed and stay up to date; they should ask insightful questions and be active participants in the oversight function.

Specific areas of accounting 'hocus-pocus' that may obscure financial volatility and adversely affect the quality of reported earnings are:

- *Revenue recognition* – recognising turnover before a sale is complete, or at a time when the customer still has options to terminate, void or delay the sale, has assumed great importance in recent years. This is particularly so for 'new economy' companies where the focus is often on revenue rather than profit.
- *Changing estimates* – changing estimates to make the numbers is another frequently used method for managing earnings. While this may be perfectly acceptable when supported by real economic facts, all too often estimates are altered when the underlying economics of the business do not support the change, and without any disclosure to investors. As such, investors end up using numbers for investment decisions that lack transparency, consistency and comparability.
- *Abuse of the materiality concept* – the intentional recording of errors under the assertion that their impact on the bottom line is not significant; however, given the market's reaction to small changes in earnings per share, what is significant and what is not?
- *Capitalisation and deferral of expenses* – capitalising and deferring costs that should be accounted for as a cost of the period through, for example, ambiguously defined capitalisation criteria for property, plant and equipment and intangible assets, unreasonable amortisation periods, or through the capitalisation of costs for which future economic benefits are not reasonably assured.
- *Non-GAAP measures* – this is a device that some companies can use to disseminate an idealised version of their performance that excludes any number of costs and expenses yet still suggests reliability and comparability. In effect, spinning straw into gold!

Often undue emphasis is placed on results before exceptional items, or start-up operations, or earnings before interest, tax and depreciation (EBITDA), and even marketing expenses, as if some costs were somehow capable of being ignored. This may be perfectly appropriate, and consistent with what is done in the industry, but the impression given can be of a lack of balance.

5 Overseeing financial risks and internal control processes

The audit committee's second oversight responsibility relates to the company's financial risk and internal control processes. This is an area which some audit committees find challenging, because it appears to encompass a broad and difficult subject. In practice the most effective audit committees approach this issue by demanding relevant, timely and accurate information from senior management, internal audit, and the external auditor, and by asking direct and challenging questions.

Overseeing the process related to the company's financial risks

Risk management involves identifying risks that may prevent a company from achieving its objectives, analysing those risks, avoiding certain risks, and managing the risks that remain. The board of directors is ultimately responsible for the risk management system and for reviewing its effectiveness. The company's management is responsible for the identification, assessment and monitoring of risk, for developing, operating and monitoring the system of internal control and for providing assurance to the board that it has done so.

The process related to identifying and managing the company's risks, as a part of the company's overall control environment, influences the identification and management of financial risks that can affect the company's financial reporting – a matter of critical importance to the audit committee.

> The audit committee should review the company's internal financial controls (that is, the systems established to identify, assess, manage and monitor financial risks).
>
> *Smith Guidance*

The audit committee, as a committee appointed by the board of directors, is responsible for assisting the board in fulfilling its oversight responsibilities. In particular, the audit committee's primary duties and responsibilities are to monitor the management of the principal risks that could impact the financial reporting process of the company, monitor the integrity of the system of internal controls regarding financial reporting and accounting compliance, and oversee the internal and external audit process.

In addition to their direct oversight responsibilities for risks affecting financial reporting, audit committees are sometimes asked by the board to examine objectively the degree to which management has assumed 'ownership' for overall risk management, the appropriateness of the risk management strategy and process adopted in addressing this responsibility, and the adequacy and effectiveness of systems to support the process.

By asking probing questions about risk management, the audit committee can help bring clarity to the process used to manage risk and the assignment of account-abilities to monitor and react to changes in the organisation's risk profile.

Appendix 8 contains a number of high-level questions the audit committee may like to consider in framing such discussions with management.

Overseeing internal control

An effective control environment needs more than good controls; it needs competent oversight. Management, internal auditors, external auditors and the audit committee each have roles in ensuring that an effective control environment exists.

The audit committee is responsible for overseeing the financial reporting process, including the risks and controls in that process. Internal control, however, encompasses not only financial reporting but also compliance with laws and regulations and operational control. The board is responsible for the overall risks and controls of the company and, therefore, has the discretion to give the audit committee responsibility for oversight of compliance with laws and regulations and operational controls. Indeed, the Smith Guidance suggests that the audit committee should review the wider aspects of internal control and risk management systems, unless expressly addressed by the board or a separate risk committee comprised of independent directors.[1] Furthermore, except to the extent that this is expressly dealt with by the board or risk committee, the audit committee should review and approve any statements included in the annual report in relation to internal control and the management of risk.

> Except where the board or a risk committee is expressly responsible for reviewing the effectiveness of the internal control and risk management systems, the audit committee should receive reports from management on the effectiveness of the systems they have established and the conclusions of any testing carried out by internal and external auditors.
>
> *Smith Guidance*

---

[1] It should be noted that the Smith Guidance refers to risk committees comprised solely of independent directors – not, as is more common in the UK, executive risk committees. While management clearly has the major role in the risk management framework, it is not an oversight role. This should properly be carried out by the board as a whole (or a committee comprised of independent directors if the board delegates its obligations under the Smith Guidance).

There is a tension here between the role of the audit committee as articulated in the Smith Report and the ICAEW guidance *Internal Control: Guidance for directors on the Combined Code* (the Turnbull Report) which expressly states that 'reviewing the effectiveness of internal control is an essential part of the board's responsibilities' and that 'the board takes responsibility for the disclosures on internal control in the annual report and accounts.' Turnbull does not preclude the audit committee from carrying aspects of the board's review work; however, the results of the committee's work should be reported to, and considered by, the board prior to the board reaching its own conclusions.

Turnbull's report goes on to clarify the role of board committees in the review process. It states that the role of such committees, including the audit committee, 'is for the board to decide and will depend upon factors such as the size and composition of the board; the scale, diversity and complexity of the company's operations; and the nature of the significant risks that the company faces.' It is imperative that audit committees ensure they understand any responsibilities they have for internal controls beyond those related to financial reporting.

Management is responsible for designing and implementing an effective system of internal control. The audit committee must determine that management has implemented policies that ensure the company's risks around financial reporting (and, where applicable, the wider sphere of business risk) are identified and that controls are adequate, in place, and functioning properly. As part of its assessment, the audit committee should consider requesting from management an overview of the risks, policies, procedures, and controls surrounding the integrity of financial reporting. However, the committee should strive to ensure that the information it receives is manageable – it should not be so voluminous as to deter a proper understanding of the key risks. It is more important that the audit committee gains meaningful insight into the key sources of risk and how such risks are managed, and responds with pertinent challenge than be presented with a complete, register of every conceivable risk facing the business.

A key question the audit committee can ask is: 'What changes have there been, and why?' Within a competitive market place, a business has to accept more risk, or at least adjust the range and degree of risk within the business (i.e. the risk portfolio) merely to stand still!

An example risk summary and register focused on a small number of key risks is included at Appendix 14. Such a summary is designed to give audit committee members a quick insight into the key risks and the effectiveness of the controls in place.

The audit committee should supplement representations received from management with further information and assurance from the internal and external auditors.

The integrity and attitude of senior management and the board of directors, including its committees (referred to as the 'tone at the top') is the most important factor contributing to the integrity of internal controls, including those surrounding the financial reporting process. The 'tone at the top' becomes the cultural core of the company and a model of appropriate conduct for every level. The committee should annually evaluate whether management is setting, documenting and communicating the appropriate tone. To facilitate the review, the committee should consider requesting updates and briefings from management and others on how compliance with ethical policies and other relevant company procedures is being achieved.

Whistleblowing

Audit committee members are not involved in the day-to-day management of the company and therefore will not be close enough on an on-going basis to the detail on matters related to fraud and unethical activities. The audit committee can, however, usefully focus attention on the need for proper policies and procedures to help prevent fraud and unethical activities. It is worth noting at this point that improprieties and malpractice will not necessarily be restricted to financial and accounting matters. Corporate failures in other areas, such as those relating to product quality, the safety of employees and the general public, and protection of the environment may also damage the company's reputation.

The audit committee's objective should be to ensure that appropriate arrangements are in place to enable employees to report, in confidence, possible improprieties. The audit committee should have a basic understanding of the relevant sections of the Public Interest Disclosure Act 1998 which gave protection from victimisation and dismissal to individuals who make certain disclosures in the public interest. The ICSA's Best Practice Guide on Establishing a Whistleblowing Procedure is shown in Appendix 10. The Guide provides commentary on the Act and guidance on the essential features of internal whistleblowing procedures.

The audit committee is specifically charged with ensuring that the company has arrangements for the proportionate and independent investigation of any concerns about possible improprieties raised and that appropriate follow-up action is taken.

> The audit committee should review arrangements by which staff may raise concerns about possible improprieties in matters of financial reporting or other matters.
>
> *Smith Guidance*

The Smith Guidance states that audit committees should review arrangements by which employees may, in confidence, raise concerns about possible improprieties in matters of financial reporting and other matters – in short, ensure that appropriate whistleblowing policies and procedures are in place.

When reviewing whistleblowing procedures, the committee should consider the following:

- Are whistleblowing procedures documented and communicated throughout the organisation?

- Does the policy make clear that it is both safe and acceptable for employees to raise concerns about wrongdoing?
- Were whistleblowing procedures arrived at through a consultative process? Do employees buy-in to the process?
- Are concerns that have been raised by employees responded to within a reasonable timeframe?
- Are procedures in place to ensure all reasonable steps are taken to prevent the victimisation of genuine whistleblowers?
- Are there procedures to ensure all reasonable steps are taken to safeguard the confidentiality of whistleblowers?
- Has account been taken of confidentiality clauses in contracts of employment?
- Has a senior person been identified to whom confidential concerns can be disclosed? Does this person have the authority and determination to act if concerns are not raised with – or properly dealt with by – immediate line management?
- Are success stories publicised?
- Do managers understand how to act if a concern is raised? Do they understand that employees have the right to blow the whistle?
- Has consideration been given to the use of an independent advice centre as part of the whistleblowing procedure?

Appendix 10 contains an example of a whistleblowing policy. This is also included on the accompanying CD.

Emerging issues

The following sections outline emerging issues which audit committee members ought to be aware of in order to carry out fully their responsibility as overall guardians of financial integrity for the shareholders.

Enterprise risk management

Is the board of directors adequately overseeing management's process for identifying and monitoring principal business risks? What risks are acceptable to the company, and through what process are they being managed? Is enterprise risk management being used to manage an organisation's key business risks and opportunities with the intent of maximising shareholder value?

As business leaders seek new ways to build shareholder value, they are discovering a connection between value management and risk management. Enterprise risk management (ERM) has emerged as an important means of identifying the critical risks the organisation faces – including, for example, reputation, ethics, e-business and health, safety and environmental risks (not just financial or insurable hazards)

– and then managing and optimising that portfolio of risks such that commensurate financial rewards are realized.

Business risks that are not managed have clear consequences for an organization – potential shareholder wealth erosion, exposure to the viability and success of the organisation, and exposure to financial consequences of unexpected events – all of which can affect a company's financial reporting. ERM can provide businesses with tools for monitoring the processes in place to identify significant business risks at the organisation, ensuring that those risks are being managed and reporting the organisation's risk management activities to shareholders.

Emerging ERM model

Early models of risk management viewed risk as a market imperative – something to be understood and analysed for its own sake. The new models are clearly linked to the organisation's business strategy, which encompasses an organisation's vision, mission and objectives; its process for defining operational imperatives; and its philosophies, policies, plans and initiatives for growth and development. Emerging ERM models, such as the one outlined below, can provide an organisation with new action steps that they may use to enhance business decision-making and, potentially, shareholder value.

- *Risk strategy.* Aligning ERM resources and actions with the business strategy is necessary in order to maximise organisational effectiveness. Both the board and senior management must understand strategic-level risks and related systems of control. Risk management should always be on the board's agenda and, where appropriate, that of the audit committee, and a formal risk and control review should be performed at least annually.

- *Risk portfolio.* A 'risk portfolio' represents the range and degree of business risks appropriate for the organisation at any given time. Processes must determine whether the risk portfolio is consistent with the expectations of the board and senior management.

- *Risk optimisation.* An appropriate level of risk can help achieve corporate objectives. Risk optimisation involves evaluating and adjusting the risk response currently being made by the organisation. When benchmarked against risk appetite, an optimisation model can identify where the best 'return on control investment' can be achieved.

- *Measuring and monitoring.* Measuring and monitoring to enhance value should be an ongoing means of understanding and reporting on the status and impact of risks. A strong process for capturing information and reporting it to the board and, where appropriate, audit committee, is essential to an ERM approach. Measuring and monitoring activities could include using performance measures, tracking risk management investment, using the internal audit function as an objective quality assurance yardstick and use of technology to access key business indicators.

- *Risk structure.* Once an organisation understands its risk strategy and gives risk 'top-down' priority, the organisational structure must often be adjusted to ensure that it can respond. For example, a well-defined risk structure will incorporate an assessment structure, where management is able to assess risks across the organisation's divisions, regions, functions and hierarchy.

How can the audit committee help in this regard? Audit committees can assist the board and management through its diagnosis of risk management activities. By asking probing questions in regard to risk management, the audit committee can help bring clarity to the assessment of the processes used to manage risk:

- Is risk management always on the board agenda? Has ERM education been provided at the board level? Is there clear 'ownership' of risk management oversight by the board?
- Has management created a high-level risk strategy (policy) aligned with strategic business objectives? Has a risk management framework been established with clear reporting lines and assignment of responsibilities for risk management?
- Does the company have a common risk culture, including the use of common risk language and concepts? Does communication about risk make use of appropriate channels and technology?
- Are risk management activities embedded into ongoing business processes?
- Are appropriate measurements and monitoring of risks being performed? Have key performance indicators (KPIs) and critical success factors related to risk been identified and success measures for risk strategy and activities established?

Risk indicators

Is the audit committee contributing to a 'no surprises' environment? Is the audit committee alert to the indicators contributing to the company's risk profile?

The environment in which an organisation operates can have a direct impact on the way a company is managed. By understanding the environment and the pressures the organisation and its management are facing, the audit committee can evaluate whether risks are being identified and, most important, being mitigated. Such an approach enables the committee to exercise its responsibilities in an active rather than a reactive manner, and minimises 'surprises'.

What influences the company's environment?

Every company is different and will be subject to its own risks, but the risks will be driven by a number of basic factors. The interaction of many elements – the organisation's control environment; management's capabilities; the industry, market conditions and expectations; the organisation's operating and financial stability; and the nature of its assets – all contribute to a unique risk profile. This profile directly affects the audit committee's core responsibilities: assessing the company's processes relating to its risks and control environment, overseeing its financial reporting, and evaluating its internal and independent audit processes.

What are the indicators to look for?

Some examples are contained in the box below. To facilitate identifying risk indicators, the company's senior executives should report regularly to the audit committee and board of directors to keep them informed of the risks and exposures facing the company. In addition, the committee should be briefed on the company's strategic objectives, procedures for achieving them, and evaluations of the progress toward meeting them. Such meetings will often be at the full board level; however, where appropriate, audit committees should request additional meetings to address issues of importance to their responsibilities, or to obtain a more detailed understanding. The committee should also seek the observations of the internal and external auditors, and draw upon its members' own business acumen.

Examples of risk indicators

- Inappropriate 'tone at the top'.
- Frequent organisational changes.
- High turnover of senior management.
- Lack of succession plans.
- Inexperienced management.
- Lack of management oversight.
- Management override.
- Autocratic management.
- Untimely reporting and responses to audit committee inquiries.
- Excessive or inappropriate performance-based compensation.
- Unrealistic earnings expectations by the financial community.
- Over-ambitious growth goals.
- Unusually rapid growth.
- Inappropriate focus on the importance of maintaining trends and achieving forecasts.
- Unusual results or trends.
- Lack of transparency in the business model and purposes of transactions.
- Exposure to rapid technological changes.
- Industry 'softness' or downturns.
- Interest rate and currency exposures.
- Overly complex organisational structures or transactions.
- Late surprises.
- Ongoing or prior investigations by regulators or others.

Fraud and illegal acts

Is the audit committee alert to factors increasing the risk of fraud and illegal acts? Does the audit committee understand how to minimise the risk of loss arising from fraud?

The nature of fraud risk is changing. The globalisation of business means that management may find it is doing business with people it doesn't know in countries it has never visited, employing cultural standards it doesn't understand. Technological advances have changed the speed and ways in which business transactions are recorded; these advances have enhanced opportunities for fraud and have greatly increased the potential quantum of losses arising from fraud.

How can the audit committee ensure that appropriate procedures are in place to minimise the risk of losses arising from fraud?

Unpalatable though it may be, the audit committee has to address the risk of fraud head-on. The identification of the risk of losses arising from fraud through diagnostic studies of the risk of fraud and misconduct in the business should be considered an important first step. The audit committee should question whether management has considered those risks likely to have greatest financial, reputational or regulatory impact on the business. The assessment should include identifying fraud risks and a rigorous assessment of any relevant internal controls and their ability to prevent and or detect fraud.

The audit committee should determine whether a consistent approach is taken across the business, whether those risks assessed as high are dealt with appropriately and whether management is engaged in the process.

It is important that staff at all levels receive some training in fraud awareness relevant to their business sector. A common theme arising from the investigation of many frauds is the fact that countless people in the affected organisation knew or suspected that irregularities were occurring, but were not given the skills to identify the signs of fraud, or provided with an opportunity to communicate their concerns. The committee should enquire as to whether the company has an effective awareness programme which is updated as appropriate and is provided in a relevant format to different levels of management and staff (including new joiners).

As previously discussed, the audit committee is not closely involved with the detail on matters related to fraud and unethical activities, but it can usefully focus its attention on the policies and procedures to help prevent fraud and unethical activities. The committee should question whether appropriate policies have been issued and whether they are user-friendly and adopted by all relevant business units. Polices which might be considered include a fraud response plan and a whistleblowing policy (see page 28). The committee should consider not just whether these are appropriate but whether they are effective and how the business units have confirmed this. The audit committee's objective should be to ensure that arrangements are in place for the proportionate and independent investigation of such matters and for appropriate follow-up action – therefore an oversight role.

The committee should ensure management is providing clear direction to the business on fraud and are requesting and receiving relevant information on suspected fraud and risks.

The following are, among other factors, sometimes seen as symptomatic of a potential for fraud to occur:

- an overly dominant chief executive with unfettered powers;
- frequent changes in finance or other directors, auditors or other professional advisers;
- implausible explanations as to the source of profits, or projections that are too good to be true;
- individuals who have expensive lifestyles or habits that seem at variance with the remuneration they receive from the company;
- people who have a reputation for 'sharp' practices; and
- over-complicated corporate structures involving havens of secrecy.

Complex corporate structures

Do the processes and controls adequately support the organisation's complexity and international reach? Are controls and systems keeping pace with the company's growth?

Mergers, acquisitions and reorganisations often involve melding organisations not only with distinct corporate cultures but also from different industries and different areas of the world. In today's business environment, companies frequently cross borders for every aspect of their business. This environment presents management and the audit committee with unique oversight challenges. While governance practices in such environments are slowly evolving, the influence of global business needs to be carefully considered. A number of questions may need answering:

- How are management's reporting, control, and compliance responsibilities integrated?
- Is there effective oversight of local boards?
- How does the committee evaluate domestic and international audit results, both internal and independent?
- How does management ensure compliance with various countries' rules and regulations?

Reorganisations can often mean downsizing and outsourcing. When downsizing, controls are often removed or weakened. As companies focus on core competencies, non-core activities and specialised skills are often outsourced to third-party providers.

- Has the organisation carefully evaluated the ongoing internal control impact of such decisions?

Audit committees' responsibilities do not stop at national or organizational boundaries – they extend to the company as a whole. There needs to be coordination and communication between audit committees of parent companies and subsidiaries. There should be a common appreciation of the control frameworks and cultures of the entities, and substantial sharing of information.

Emerging companies

Are any dominant entrepreneurs adequately governed? Fast-growing entrepreneurial companies often lack a formalised management structure and may not have well-established corporate governance programmes. Policies, procedures, and processes may be evolving haphazardly to meet demands. The dominant role of an individual executive also may overshadow the need to foster a strong control environment and can potentially affect the financial reporting and audit processes.

As companies grow, a more standardised corporate governance process becomes a necessity, regardless of the entity's public aspirations. For companies considering an initial public offering, the need for a formalised structure becomes obvious. While the risks described in this publication represent important issues in today's marketplace for public companies, they also apply to entrepreneurial and other companies that remain private. Responding to these risks is equally important to companies that wish to deter fraud and improve the quality of their financial reporting.

Dominant or autocratic management can also be a cause for concern in an established company. Such leadership can put a strain on the enterprise's controls and corporate governance processes and set the wrong 'tone at the top'. Ensuring that management fosters an atmosphere that supports a strong control environment is a core audit committee responsibility.

Specialised and regulated industries

Does the audit committee tailor its responsibilities to reflect specific industry considerations? Has management addressed specific industry regulations and requirements? What is the relationship between the audit committee and industry regulators.

Companies may operate in one or several industries. The more diverse the company, the more attuned the audit committee should be to different industry risks, accounting practices, laws, regulations, and reporting and disclosure requirements. An audit committee must consider management's response to the risks inherent in these specialised practices and incorporate them into its agenda. While the core responsibilities described in this publication are relevant to most audit committees, the manner of their execution and the specifics of audit committee activities should be tailored to meet the needs of each specific industry. An understanding of the industry and the organisation will enable the audit committee member to identify and react to industry-specific requirements such as those in depository institutions, health care organisations, not-for-profit organisations, investment companies, insurance companies, or governmental entities.

In considering industries that are regulated, audit committees should be acquainted with the scope of the regulation and the authority of the regulators. They should understand the demands regulators place upon the business, and management's attitude towards them and relationship with them.

6 Overseeing the internal and external audit processes

The audit committee's final responsibility is to oversee the internal and external audit processes. The Smith Guidance addresses the five key elements of the relationship between auditor and the audit committee: the appointment of the auditors, their approach to the audit, the outcomes from their work, regular assessment of their performance and the maintenance of their independence.

Internal auditors' oversight

Companies often need to weigh the benefits and costs of internal control considerations. One such decision often relates to the need or desirability of having an internal audit function. Internal audit functions, designed and deployed effectively, can have a very positive impact on the control environment of a company and the effective design and operation of internal controls.

> The audit committee should monitor and review the effectiveness of the company's internal audit function. Where there is no internal audit function, the audit committee should consider annually whether there is a need for such a function.
>
> *Smith Guidance*

As an important aspect of its mandate, internal audit can provide the audit committee with a means of monitoring whether the controls management has put in place are reliable, functioning properly and sufficient to address the risks in the financial reporting process. Accordingly, the audit committee should review the need for an internal audit function, and where such a function exists, its effectiveness.

> When reviewing the internal audit function's remit, the audit committee should have regard to the complementary roles of the internal and external audit functions.
>
> *Smith Guidance*

If a company has an internal audit function, both the internal audit department and the external audit firm execute a company's audit coverage. While each has its own unique responsibilities, the audit committee should ensure that they complement each other, that their audit effort is coordinated and that there is effective communication between them. The external auditor is responsible for auditing and attesting to the company's financial statements; the internal auditor, inter alia, for monitoring the performance of a company's internal controls. The external auditor should identify the internal audit activities that are relevant to planning the external audit.

Where an internal audit function exists, the audit committee should participate in the appointment, promotion, or dismissal of the head of internal audit, and help determine his or her qualifications, reporting hierarchy – to ensure access to all necessary contacts both at the board level and within the organisation – and compensation.

> The audit committee should approve the appointment or termination of appointment of the head of internal audit.
>
> *Smith Guidance*

The audit committee should be involved in developing and approving the internal audit department's mandate, goals and mission, to be certain of its proper role in the oversight function. A collaborative effort with both management and internal audit in the development of the internal audit mandate often helps ensure a proper balance between the assessment of internal controls related to financial reporting and other special projects, operational efficiency and risk management responsibilities. A specimen internal audit plan is included in Appendix 13 and on the accompanying CD.

> The audit committee should ensure that the internal audit function has the necessary resources and access to information to enable it to fulfil its mandate, and is equipped to perform in accordance with appropriate professional standards.
>
> *Smith Guidance*

The audit committee should also be satisfied that the internal audit function has adequate resources. The committee should stay up to date on the scope and results of the department's operations and management's responses to the department's recommendations on internal controls and compliance. The department's objectivity and independence of judgement should be periodically evaluated. The committee should monitor and assess the role and effectiveness of the internal audit function in the overall context of the company's risk management system and, in particular, ensure that the internal audit department's involvement in the financial reporting process is appropriate.

Self-assessment by the head of internal audit is an effective assessment tool, but it should not be the sole means by which the effectiveness of the internal audit function is reviewed. The committee should draw its own conclusions based on its experience of and contact with the internal audit function. Appendix 6 provides a framework which audit committees can adapt when reviewing the effectiveness of the internal audit function.

In monitoring the work of the internal audit function, the audit committee should review and assess the annual internal audit work plan; receive a report on the results of the internal auditor's work on a periodic basis; and review and monitor management's responsiveness to the internal auditor's findings and recommendations.

Recognising the important role of internal audit and its changing activities in today's business environment, the audit committee should also consider the following issues as it oversees the internal audit function:

- How does the internal audit department best add value to the business model?
- How effectively does the company use the internal audit department to evaluate management's response to its strategic, financial, technological, security, and operational risks?
- Should the internal audit department be driving process improvements and best practices sharing? Is it?
- Is internal audit a training ground for future leaders?
- Does the internal audit department have the resources and appropriate expertise to satisfy its responsibilities?
- Would the company's objectives for the internal audit function be better served or supplemented through the use of a third-party service provider?

> The audit committee should ensure that the internal auditor has direct access to the board chairman and to the audit committee and is accountable to the audit committee.
>
> *Smith Guidance*

The internal auditor is in the unique position of being employed by management yet is expected to review its conduct. The audit committee should have mechanisms in place to facilitate confidential exchanges with the internal auditor, with regular meetings scheduled between the audit committee and the internal auditor.

Today's internal audit functions generally apply a risk-based methodology, and have access to the specialised skills necessary to deal with complex treasury, technology and operational strategies being employed by the company.

External auditors' oversight

First and foremost, the external auditor and audit committee should have a strong and candid relationship – anything less may limit the committee's effectiveness in achieving its oversight responsibilities. The audit committee should ensure that the external auditors are accountable to the audit committee – and through them, to the board of directors and ultimately the company's members. The audit committee should ensure its actions and communications with the external auditor are consistent with this accountability. The audit committee should also ensure that they communicate their expectations to the external auditor, and that both parties understand and have agreed to those expectations.

Appointment, reappointment and removal

> The audit committee should have primary responsibility for making a recommendation on the appointment, reappointment and removal of the external auditors.
>
> *Smith Guidance*

Making recommendations to the board on the appointment, reappointment and removal of the external auditors is an important audit committee responsibility. The audit committee's recommendation to the board should be based on its assessment of the qualification, expertise, resources and independence of the external auditors and the effectiveness of the audit process. The assessment should cover all aspects of the audit service provided by the audit firm, and include obtaining a report on the audit firm's own internal quality control procedures. If the audit committee recommends considering the selection of possible new appointees as external auditors, it should oversee the selection process.

The audit committee should approve the terms of engagement and recommend the remuneration to be paid to the external auditor in respect of audit services provided. In doing so, it should satisfy itself that the level of fee payable in respect of the external audit is appropriate and that an effective audit can be conducted for such a fee.

In the unlikely event that the board does not accept the audit committee's recommendation regarding the appointment/reappointment of the auditor, compliance with the Combined Code requires it to include in the annual report, and in any papers recommending the appointment or reappointment of the auditor, a statement from the audit committee explaining its recommendation and the reasons why the board has taken a different position.

If the external auditor resigns, the audit committee should investigate the issues giving rise to such resignation and consider whether any action is required.

Independence

> The audit committee should have procedures to ensure the independence and objectivity of the external auditor and should seek reassurance that the auditors and their staff have no family, financial, employment, investment or business relationship with the company.
>
> *Smith Guidance*

The audit committee should consider the auditor's independence and annually carry out procedures to ensure the independence and objectivity of the external auditor, taking into consideration relevant UK professional and regulatory requirements. For their part, all auditing firms should have internal policies and procedures in place and properly monitored to ensure that the audit firm and its individual members are independent from the company.

In considering matters that may bear on the auditor's independence, both the auditor and the audit committee should consider whether conflicts exist, such as the auditor holding a financial interest, either directly or indirectly, in the company; personal and business relationships of the auditor's immediate family, close relatives and partners with the company; economic dependence by the auditor through their relationship with the company; and the nature and extent of services provided by the auditor in addition to the audit engagement. Each year the audit committee should seek from the audit firm information about policies and processes for maintaining independence and monitoring compliance with relevant requirements, including current requirements regarding the rotation of audit partners and staff.

Communications from external auditors

Statement of Auditing Standard 610 *Communication of audit matters to those charged with governance* (SAS 610) requires that, inter alia, for all audit engagements where the audited entity is a listed company, at least annually the auditor should:

(a) disclose in writing to the audit committee, and discuss as appropriate:
  - all relationships between the audit firm and its related entities and the client entity and its related entities that may reasonably be thought to bear on the firm's independence and the objectivity of the audit engagement partner and the audit staff; and
  - the related safeguards that are in place; and

(b) where this is the case, confirm in writing to the audit committee that, in their professional judgement, the firm is independent within the meaning of regulatory and professional requirements and the objectivity of the audit engagement partner and audit staff is not impaired.

The audit committee should agree with the board a policy for the employment of former employees of the external auditor, taking into account the relevant ethical guidelines governing the accounting profession. Particular attention should be paid to those individuals who were part of the audit team and moved directly to the company. The audit committee should monitor application of the policy, including the number of former employees of the external auditor currently employed in senior positions in the company, and consider whether in the light of this there has been any impairment, or appearance of impairment, of the auditor's judgement or independence. Appendix 11 contains an example policy on the employment of former employees of the external auditor.

The audit committee should also monitor the external auditor's compliance with UK ethical guidance relating to the rotation of audit partners, the level of fees that the company pays in proportion to the overall fee income of the firm, office and partner, and other related regulatory requirements.

> The audit committee should develop and recommend to the board the company's policy in relation to the provision of non-audit services by the auditor.
>
> *Smith Guidance*

To ensure that non-audit services provided by the auditor do not impair, or appear to impair, the auditor's independence or objectivity, the audit committee should develop, and recommend to the board, a policy in relation to the provision of non-audit services. In determining the policy, the audit committee should consider the skills and experience of the audit firm; the potential threats to the auditor's independence and objectivity; and any controls put in place by the auditor to mitigate such threats.

> Audit committees should consider:
> – whether the skills and experience of the audit firm make it a suitable supplier;
> – whether there are safeguards in place to ensure that there is no threat to objectivity and independence;
> – the nature of the non-audit services, the related fee levels; and
> – the criteria which govern the compensation of the individuals performing the audit.
>
> *Smith Guidance*

In principle, the audit committee should not agree to the auditor providing a service if the result is that:

- the auditor has a financial or other interest which might cause them to be reluctant to take actions that would be adverse to the interests of the audit firm (self-interest);
- the results of the non-audit service performed by the auditor may be included in the accounts, and thus not subject to proper review (self-review);
- the auditor undertakes work that involves making judgements and taking decisions which are the responsibility of management (management);
- the auditor undertakes work that involves acting as advocate for the company (advocacy);
- the auditor is predisposed to accept or not sufficiently question the company's point of view (familiarity); or
- the auditor's conduct may be influenced by fear or threats (intimidation).

The policy devised by the audit committee should formally specify the types of non-audit work from which the external auditors should be excluded; the type of work for which the external auditors can be engaged without referral to the audit committee; and the type of work for which a case-by-case decision is necessary. Where non-audit services require approval on a case-by-case basis, it may be appropriate for the policy to allow 'pre-approval' for certain types for work, subject to a fee limit determined by the audit committee. The subsequent provision of any service by the auditor should be ratified at the next meeting of the audit committee. More generally, a de minimis fee limit might apply. Appendix 7 contains an example policy in respect of the appointment and remuneration of external auditors for non-audit work.

Understanding the audit cycle

Once an external auditor has been appointed, the audit committee should review and agree the audit engagement letter, ensuring that it has been updated to reflect changes in circumstances arising since the previous year (or previous auditor). Where there has been a change in auditor, all material issues should, in practice, have been addressed during the appointment process.

> The audit committee should review the scope of the external audit with the auditor. If the committee is not satisfied as to its adequacy it should arrange for additional work to be undertaken.
>
> *Smith Guidance*

The committee needs to understand the scope of the audit and how it is to be approached. An effective way to achieve this is to hold a pre-audit meeting with the auditors. Audit committees can sometimes have a limited appreciation of what it is the auditors actually do. An open discussion around this topic can throw up quite a number of areas where the audit committee assumes work is done where it isn't, and where audit effort is directed and the audit committee has absolutely no appreciation of it. Audit committees should have an interest in the areas of detailed substantive testing which the auditors intend to carry out and on the other hand those where they intend to rely on internal control and the means by which they justify that reliance. The committee should also be concerned that there is adequate coverage of (say) divisions or subsidiaries, particularly those that are remote either geographically or culturally.

After the pre-audit meeting, the committee may determine that the external auditors should be performing additional work to satisfy the needs of the company, such as increased internal control testing. The process may also help the audit committee understand and coordinate activities with the internal auditors.

The committee should also ensure that an appropriate audit plan is in place. A proper dialogue needs to take place as to whether the business risks identified by the auditor are the only business risks, or whether there are other risks that should be taken account of in view of the audit committee's own knowledge of the company's risk environment. This applies both at a strategic level – those risks which are fundamental to the achievement of the company's strategy – and at the more detailed operational level – those risks which impact the day-to-day operations, the recognition of revenue and cost, the custody and value of assets and completeness of recognition of liabilities.

> The committee should consider whether planned levels of materiality and proposed audit resources are consistent with the scope of the audit, having regard also to the seniority, expertise and experience of the audit team.
>
> *Smith Guidance*

Moving to the end of the audit cycle, the audit committee should oversee the audit findings, including any changes in audit approach or any modification to the standard auditor's report. The issues to be discussed will depend on individual company and audit circumstances. Nevertheless, the audit committee should:

- discuss with the external auditor major issues that arose during the course of the audit and have subsequently been resolved and those issues that have been left unresolved;
- review key accounting and audit judgements; and
- review levels of errors identified during the audit, obtaining explanations from management and, where necessary the external auditor, as to why certain errors might remain unadjusted.

Sufficient time should be allowed to enable the audit committee to complete its review and engage in an appropriate dialogue with the external auditor. An appropriate timetable should be agreed with the board, finance director and the auditor.

This is all very much common sense but, in practice, major issues should not be raised for the first time at the meeting at which the committee intend to recommend the approval of the financial statements. If the final audit committee meeting is to be conducted effectively, it is advisable that audit findings are reviewed on an ongoing and timely basis (for example, after the interim audit work). Issues can then be identified at an early stage, and surprises avoided. Audit committee chairmen should consider entering into a regular dialogue with the auditor in advance of the final meeting so that the attention of the audit committee members can be directed to matters of concern, rather than cantering through the agenda. One would expect the relationship with the auditor to be such that if there are serious concerns, these are brought to the audit committee's attention promptly.

Communications from external auditors

Statement of Auditing Standard 610 formalises auditors' communication with those charged with governance in respect of the financial reporting process – for listed companies, this will usually be the audit committee.

Adjustment of errors. SAS 610 requires auditors to bring to the attention of those charged with governance any unadjusted misstatements in the accounts, other than those that are 'clearly trifling'. A representation is also to be sought from directors about their reasons for not correcting the relevant matters.

Qualitative aspects of financial reporting. Auditors are required to discuss, in an open and frank manner, the quality and acceptability of the entity's reporting, including for example:

- the appropriateness of the accounting policies to the particular circumstances of the company;
- the timing of transactions and the period in which they are recorded;
- the appropriateness of accounting estimates and judgements made;
- the potential impact of any uncertainties including significant risks and exposures, such as pending litigation;
- material uncertainties that may cast doubt on the company's ability to continue as a going concern;
- the extent to which the accounts are affected by unusual transactions including non-recurring profits;
- inconsistencies between the accounts and other information in the document containing the accounts; and
- the overall balance and clarity of the annual report.

While it may seem strange to review issues that have subsequently been resolved and unadjusted errors that are not material, such issues could suggest weaknesses in the design or operation of internal controls, or be indicative of management's approach to the preparation and presentation of financial information (e.g. earnings management).

During an audit, many representations are made to the auditors, either unsolicited or in response to specific enquiries. The audit committee should review such representations before signature by management. Representation letters cover matters such as:

- confirmation that all accounting records have been made available, all transactions properly recorded in the accounting records, and all other records and related information made available;
- the directors' expectations regarding future events that affect critical accounting judgements, for example, the recoverability of debtors; and
- the company's expectations and future intentions.

Particular consideration should be given to matters that relate to non-standard issues. The audit committee should consider whether the information provided is complete and appropriate based on its own knowledge.

Where the auditors identify material weaknesses in either accounting or internal control systems during their audit report, they report these to the company in a 'management letter'. As part of the ongoing monitoring process, the audit committee should review the management letter and also review and monitor management's responsiveness to the external auditor's findings and recommendations.

Assessment of the external auditor

The audit committee has primary responsibility for selecting, evaluating, and, if need be, replacing the auditor. The committee's evaluation should consider the auditor's competence, the quality and efficiency of the audit, and whether the audit fee is appropriate in relation to the size, complexity, and risk and control profile of the company to ensure that the company's audit is not compromised.

> The audit committee should assess annually the qualification, expertise and resources, and independence of the external auditor and the effectiveness of the audit process. The assessment should cover all aspects of the audit service provided by the audit firm, and include obtaining a report on the audit firm's own internal quality control procedures.
>
> *Smith Guidance*

The Combined Code recommends that the audit committee should review and monitor the external auditor's independence and objectivity and the effectiveness of the audit process, taking into consideration relevant UK professional and regulatory requirements. The Smith Guidance builds on this recommendation by further recommending that the audit committee assess the effectiveness of the audit process, and in doing so:

- review whether the auditor has met the agreed audit plan and understand the reasons for any changes, including changes in perceived audit risks and the work undertaken by the external auditor to address those risks;
- consider the robustness and perceptiveness of the auditors in their handling of the key accounting and audit judgements identified and in responding to questions from the audit committees, and in their commentary where appropriate on the systems of internal control;
- obtain feedback about the conduct of the audit from key people involved, e.g. the finance director and the head of internal audit; and
- review and monitor the content of the external auditor's management letter, in order to assess whether it is based on a good understanding of the company's business and establish whether recommendations have been acted upon and, if not, the reasons why they have not been acted upon.

Appendix 5 suggests a checklist framework for an audit committee to carry out a formal review of the effectiveness and efficiency of their external auditors. Such a review provides the audit committee with a disciplined approach to keeping the auditors' performance under review.

Disclosure

Compliance with the Combined Code requires that the audit committee's terms of reference, including its role and the authority delegated to it by the board, should be made available on request and included on the company's website. Furthermore, a separate section of the annual report should describe the work of the audit committee in discharging those duties, specifically those in relation to the external auditor. Such a report should:

- explain to shareholders how, if the auditor provides non-audit services, auditor objectivity and independence are safeguarded;
- where the board does not accept the audit committee's recommendation on the appointment or reappointment of the auditor, explain the committee's recommendation and the reasons why the board has taken a different position; and
- where no internal audit function exists, set out the reasons for the absence of such a function.

To this list, the Smith Guidance adds the number of audit committee meetings and the names and qualifications of all members of the audit committee during the period.

Specimen audit committee disclosures can be found in Appendix 12.

Appendices

Appendices

Some of the materials contained in this book are reproduced on the accompanying CD in order to provide readers with the convenience of being able to adapt and tailor documents to their own requirements.

For the convenience of readers, appendices 1–15 have been included on the accompanying CD so that they can be easily adapted to suit individual requirements.

Appendix 1
ICSA Example audit committee terms of reference

Audit committees play a critical role in a Company's financial reporting system by overseeing and monitoring management's and the external auditors' participation in the financial reporting process. It is expected that the preparation and disclosure of the audit committee terms of reference will help shareholders assess the role and responsibilities of the audit committee and help committee members focus on their responsibilities.

The ICSA's intention is not to advocate an exhaustive mandate. Rather, this example terms of reference is intended to help audit committees, and senior management, in evaluating the completeness of their mandates in relation to their specific circumstance. Audit committees should also be mindful of the increasing demand for disclosure of corporate governance practices. Accordingly, care in crafting the terms of reference must be exercised so that audit committees are not exposing themselves to undue liability.

All audit committees should establish terms of reference that not only meet the minimum requirements, but are also tailored to their specific needs and circumstances. Audit committees governing smaller companies, for example, may require fewer meetings per year and may not need to address certain responsibilities for oversight of internal audit or monitoring compliance with a code of ethics if these items are not a part of the Company's governance structure. Accordingly, the terms of reference should be 'tailored fit' to the circumstances of the entity.

The following terms of reference have been produced by the ICSA.

Reference to 'the Committee' shall mean the Audit Committee. Reference to 'the board' shall mean the board of directors. The square brackets contain recommendations which are in line with best practice but which may need to be changed to suit the circumstances of the particular organisation.

1   Membership

1.1   Members of the Committee shall be appointed by the board, on the recommendation of the Nomination Committee in consultation with the Chairman of the Audit Committee. The Committee shall be made up of at least [3] members.

1.2   All members of the Committee shall be independent non-executive directors[1] at least one of whom shall have recent and relevant financial experience. The Chairman of the board shall not be a member of the Committee[2].

---

1 An independent non-executive director is defined in Combined Code provision A.3.1.

2 Except on appointment, the Chairman of the company is not considered to meet the test of independence. Combined Code provision A.3.1.

1.3   Only members of the Committee have the right to attend Committee meetings. However, other individuals such as the Chairman of the board, Chief Executive, Finance Director, other directors, the heads of risk, compliance and internal audit and representatives from the finance function may be invited to attend all or part of any meeting as and when appropriate.

1.4   The external auditors will be invited to attend meetings of the Committee on a regular basis.

1.5   Appointments to the Committee shall be for a period of up to three years, which may be extended for two further three-year periods, provided the director remains independent.

1.6   The board shall appoint the Committee Chairman who shall be an independent non-executive director. In the absence of the Committee Chairman and/or an appointed deputy, the remaining members present shall elect one of themselves to chair the meeting.

2   Secretary

2.1   The company secretary or their nominee shall act as the secretary of the Committee.

3   Quorum

3.1   The quorum necessary for the transaction of business shall be [2] members. A duly convened meeting of the Committee at which a quorum is present shall be competent to exercise all or any of the authorities, powers and discretions vested in or exercisable by the Committee.

4   Frequency of meetings

4.1   The Committee shall meet [at least three times a year at appropriate times in the reporting and audit cycle] [quarterly on the first Wednesday in each of January, April, July and October] and otherwise as required.[3]

5   Notice of meetings

5.1   Meetings of the Committee shall be summoned by the secretary of the Committee at the request of any of its members or at the request of external or internal auditors if they consider it necessary.

5.2   Unless otherwise agreed, notice of each meeting confirming the venue, time and date together with an agenda of items to be discussed, shall be forwarded to each member

---

3 The frequency and timing of meetings will differ according to the needs of the company. Meetings should be organised so that attendance is maximised (for example by timetabling them to coincide with board meetings).

of the Committee, any other person required to attend and all other non-executive directors, no later than [5] working days before the date of the meeting. Supporting papers shall be sent to Committee members and to other attendees as appropriate, at the same time.

6 Minutes of meetings

6.1 The secretary shall minute the proceedings and resolutions of all meetings of the Committee, including recording the names of those present and in attendance.

6.2 The secretary shall ascertain, at the beginning of each meeting, the existence of any conflicts of interest and minute them accordingly.

6.3 Minutes of Committee meetings shall be circulated promptly to all members of the Committee and, once agreed, to all members of the board.

7 Annual General Meeting

7.1 The Chairman of the Committee shall attend the Annual General Meeting prepared to respond to any shareholder questions on the Committee's activities.

8 Duties

The Committee should carry out the duties below for the parent company, major subsidiary undertakings and the group as a whole, as appropriate.

8.1 Financial reporting

8.1.1 The Committee shall monitor the integrity of the financial statements of the company, including its annual and interim reports, preliminary results' announcements and any other formal announcement relating to its financial performance, reviewing significant financial reporting issues and judgements which they contain. The Committee shall also review summary financial statements, significant financial returns to regulators and any financial information contained in certain other documents, such as announcements of a price sensitive nature.

8.1.2 The Committee shall review and challenge where necessary:

8.1.2.1 the consistency of, and any changes to, accounting policies both on a year on year basis and across the company/group;

8.1.2.2 the methods used to account for significant or unusual transactions where different approaches are possible;

8.1.2.3 whether the company has followed appropriate accounting standards and made appropriate estimates and judgements, taking into account the views of the external auditor;

8.1.2.4 the clarity of disclosure in the company's financial reports and the context in which statements are made; and

8.1.2.5 all material information presented with the financial statements, such as the operating and financial review and the corporate governance statement (insofar as it relates to the audit and risk management).

8.1.3 The Committee shall review the annual financial statements of the pension funds where not reviewed by the board as a whole.

8.2 Internal controls and risk management systems

The Committee shall:

8.2.1 keep under review the effectiveness of the company's internal controls and risk management systems; and

8.2.2 review and approve the statements to be included in the annual report concerning internal controls and risk management.[4]

8.3 Whistleblowing

The Committee shall review the company's arrangements for its employees to raise concerns, in confidence, about possible wrongdoing in financial reporting or other matters. The Committee shall ensure that these arrangements allow proportionate and independent investigation of such matters and appropriate follow-up action.

8.4 Internal audit

The Committee shall:

8.4.1 monitor and review the effectiveness of the company's internal audit function in the context of the company's overall risk management system[5];

8.4.2 approve the appointment and removal of the head of the internal audit function; and

8.4.3 consider and approve the remit of the internal audit function and ensure it has adequate resources and appropriate access to information to enable it to perform its function effectively and in accordance with the relevant professional standards.

The Committee shall also ensure the function has adequate standing and is free from management or other restrictions;

8.4.4 review and assess the annual internal audit plan;

8.4.5 review promptly all reports on the company from the internal auditors;

---

4 Unless this is done by the board as a whole.
5 If the company does not have an internal audit function, the Committee should consider annually whether there should be one and make recommendation to the board accordingly. The absence of such a function should be explained in the annual report.

8.4.6   review and monitor management's responsiveness to the findings and recommendations of the internal auditor; and

8.4.7   meet the head of internal audit at least once a year, without management being present, to discuss their remit and any issues arising from the internal audits carried out. In addition, the head of internal audit shall be given the right of direct access to the Chairman of the board and to the Committee.

8.5   External audit

The Committee shall:

8.5.1   consider and make recommendations to the board, to be put to shareholders for approval at the AGM, in relation to the appointment, re-appointment and removal of the company's external auditor. The Committee shall oversee the selection process for new auditors and if an auditor resigns the Committee shall investigate the issues leading to this and decide whether any action is required;

8.5.2   oversee the relationship with the external auditor including (but not limited to):

8.5.2.1 approval of their remuneration, whether fees for audit or non-audit services and that the level of fees is appropriate to enable an adequate audit to be conducted;

8.5.2.2 approval of their terms of engagement, including any engagement letter issued at the start of each audit and the scope of the audit;

8.5.2.3 assessing annually their independence and objectivity taking into account relevant [UK] professional and regulatory requirements and the relationship with the auditor as a whole, including the provision of any non-audit services;

8.5.2.4 satisfying itself that there are no relationships (such as family, employment, investment, financial or business) between the auditor and the company (other than in the ordinary course of business);

8.5.2.5 agreeing with the board a policy on the employment of former employees of the company's auditor, then monitoring the implementation of this policy;

8.5.2.6 monitoring the auditor's compliance with relevant ethical and professional guidance on the rotation of audit partners, the level of fees paid by the company compared to the overall fee income of the firm, office and partner and other related requirements; and

8.5.2.7 assessing annually their qualifications, expertise and resources and the effectiveness of the audit process which shall include a report from the external auditor on their own internal quality procedures;

8.5.3   meet regularly with the external auditor, including once at the planning stage before the audit and once after the audit at the reporting stage. The Committee shall meet the external auditor at least once a year, without management being present, to discuss their remit and any issues arising from the audit;

8.5.4   review and approve the annual audit plan and ensure that it is consistent with the scope of the audit engagement;

8.5.5   review the findings of the audit with the external auditor. This shall include, but not be limited to, the following;

8.5.5.1 a discussion of any major issues which arose during the audit;

8.5.5.2 any accounting and audit judgements; and

8.5.5.3 levels of errors identified during the audit.

The Committee shall also review the effectiveness of the audit.

8.5.6   review any representation letter(s) requested by the external auditor before they are signed by management;

8.5.7   review the management letter and management's response to the auditor's findings and recommendations; and

8.5.8   develop and implement a policy on the supply of non-audit services by the external auditor, taking into account any relevant ethical guidance on the matter.

8.6   Reporting responsibilities

8.6.1   The Committee Chairman shall report formally to the board on its proceedings after each meeting on all matters within its duties and responsibilities.

8.6.2   The Committee shall make whatever recommendations to the board it deems appropriate on any area within its remit where action or improvement is needed.

8.6.3   The Committee shall compile a report to shareholders on its activities to be included in the company's annual report.

8.7   Other matters

The Committee shall:

8.7.1   have access to sufficient resources in order to carry out its duties, including access to the company secretariat for assistance as required;

8.7.2   be provided with appropriate and timely training, both in the form of an induction programme for new members and on an ongoing basis for all members;

8.7.3   give due consideration to laws and regulations, the provisions of the Combined Code and the requirements of the UK Listing Authority's Listing Rules as appropriate;

8.7.4   be responsible for co-ordination of the internal and external auditors;

8.7.5   oversee any investigation of activities which are within its terms of reference and act as a court of the last resort; and

8.7.6   at least once a year, review its own performance, constitution and terms of reference to ensure it is operating at maximum effectiveness and recommend any changes it considers necessary to the board for approval.

9 Authority

The Committee is authorised:

9.1 to seek any information it requires from any employee of the company in order to perform its duties;

9.2 to obtain, at the company's expense, outside legal or other professional advice on any matter within its terms of reference; and

9.3 to call any employee to be questioned at a meeting of the Committee as and when required.

Appendix 2
Example audit committee agenda

A comprehensive agenda helps members stay focused on their mission. However, the nature of audit committee responsibilities and the ever-changing environment in which the company operates make it difficult to determine a set agenda for each meeting. The committee should assess what is currently important and develop its agenda accordingly.

The following topics deserve consideration when establishing the detailed agendas for the audit committee meetings during the year.

Risk assessment

- Risk management process and control (particularly financial reporting risks)
- Operating reviews
- Budget reviews
- Industry and market updates
- Review financial community expectations
- Information technology changes
- Legal briefings
- Understand senior management compensation programmes
- Executive sessions with appropriate senior management
- Current and emerging risk issues

Assess processes relating to the company's control environment

- Compliance with code of ethical conduct
- Control policies and procedures (including earnings management, error and fraud)
- Management's assessment of key third-party providers
- Internal and external auditor internal control observations and recommendations
- Compliance with specific industry regulations

Oversee financial reporting

- Financial statements and earnings releases
- Recommend approval of financial statements to board of directors
- Periodic reports and filings
- Management overview of financial results for quarter/year
- Critical accounting policies (including appropriate application of GAAP)
- Significant and unusual transactions and accounting estimates
- Current developments in auditing, accounting, reporting, and tax matters
- Executive session with senior management

Evaluate the internal and external audit processes

- Coordination of the internal and external audit effort and definition of responsibilities
- External auditors
  - Engagement letter
  - Audit engagement team
  - Independence letter
  - Consider all significant non-audit services to be performed by the external auditor
  - Scope, procedures and timing
  - Audit results
  - Audit reports
  - Quarterly review results
  - Meeting with external auditors
  - Management's responsiveness to audit results
  - Assess effectiveness
- Internal Audit Department
  - Assess need for internal auditing
  - Mandate and objectives
  - Appointment and compensation of chief auditor
  - Budget, staffing and resources
  - Scope, procedures and timing of the audits
  - Audit results
  - Audit reports
  - Meeting with internal auditors
  - Management's responsiveness to audit results
  - Assess effectiveness

Audit committee structure

- Update mandate
- Assess audit committee performance

Example audit committee meeting agenda for the year

It is important to review the completeness of the audit committee terms of reference as well as the agenda established for each meeting. This appendix provides an example of topics that could be covered in each audit committee meeting for a committee that meets four times per year.

The example relates to an organisation with a December year end.

	Scheduled meetings			
	April/ May	July/ August	October/ November	January/ February
Constitution				
Review audit committee's terms of reference	■			
Review code of conduct		■		
Assess independence, financial literacy, skills and experience of members		■	■	
Establish number of meetings for the forthcoming year			■	
Audit committee chair to establish meeting agenda and attendees required	■	■		■
Enhance financial literacy - update on current financial events	■			■
Assessment of financial information (discuss with management and external auditors where applicable)				
Review and recommend approval of annual financial statements				■
Review and recommend approval of half year financial statements		■		
Review and recommend approval of quarterly financial information	▨		▨	
External auditors				
Recommend appointment and review performance	■			
Approve audit fees and terms of engagement	■			
Consider policy in relation to non-audit services	■			
Consider objectivity/independence and obtain confirmation from auditor			■	

Review audit plan and scope of audit work

Review external audit findings

Discuss appropriateness of accounting policies, estimates and judgements

Discuss external auditors views on control environment including fraud risk management

Discuss with auditor in absence of executives and management

Ongoing communication (written/oral) of external auditor with audit committee

Internal auditors

Where no internal audit function, consider the need for an internal audit function

Recommend appointment of Head of Internal Audit and review performance

Review internal audit plan

Review significant internal audit reports and findings

Review progress on actions taken in response to the committee's representations

Discuss issues with auditor in the absence of executives and management

Other responsibilities

Consider financial risks and internal controls (and other controls if applicable)

Review progress on actions taken in response to the representations of the auditors

Review whistle blowing arrangements

Review legal and compliance developments

Review report to shareholders on role and responsibilities of the committee

Perform self-assessment of audit committee performance

Review financial personnel succession planning

Review director and officer expenses and related party transactions

Conduct special investigations and perform other activities as appropriate

Maintain minutes and report to board

Recommended timing   As required

Appendix 4
Example audit committee self-assessment

The audit committee should annually assess its own effectiveness and the adequacy of its terms of reference, work plans, and forum of discussion and communication. A suggested framework for such a review – an audit committee self-assessment – is set out below.

The results of the self-assessment and any action plans arising should be reported to the board after discussion with the chairman of the board. The board should also make its own assessment of the performance of audit committee's effectiveness on an annual basis

The self-assessment has been prepared on the basis that each audit committee member will complete it independently. The audit committee chairman would then lead discussion on the results of the questionnaire, focusing on those areas which clearly need improvement or where there is great variation in answers. Alternatively, the self assessment could be undertaken as a facilitated group activity led by the audit committee chairman or an external party.

Audit committee chairmen may wish to give more weight to some aspects of the self-assessment than others. Appropriate weighting will be influenced by a number of factors including, but not limited to:

- the committee's charter;
- the organisation's strategies and risk assessments;
- its control environment;
- the outcomes of previous self-assessments;
- the stage of maturity of the audit committee;
- the views of stakeholders on the organisation's corporate governance performance; and
- current and emerging business and economic factors.

The results of the self-assessment and any action plans arising should be reported to the board after discussion with the chairman of the board. The board should also make its own assessment of the performance of audit committee's effectiveness on an annual basis.

	Yes / No / N/A	Excellent 1	2	3	4	Poor 5	Comment
Terms of reference							
Have the audit committee's terms of reference been approved by the board?		☐	☐	☐	☐	☐	

	Yes / No / N/A	Excellent 1	2	3	4	Poor 5	Comment
Does the audit committee annually review its terms of reference and recommend any necessary changes to the board?		☐	☐	☐	☐	☐	

Do the terms of reference (audit committee charter) include:

	Yes / No / N/A	1	2	3	4	5	Comment
• monitoring the integrity of the financial statements;		☐	☐	☐	☐	☐	
• reviewing the company's internal financial control system;		☐	☐	☐	☐	☐	
• unless addressed by another board sub-committee or by the board itself, reviewing the company's risk management systems;		☐	☐	☐	☐	☐	
• monitoring and reviewing the effectiveness of the company's internal audit function;		☐	☐	☐	☐	☐	
• recommending to the board the appointment of the external auditor and approving their remuneration and terms of engagement following appointment by the shareholders in General Meeting;		☐	☐	☐	☐	☐	
• monitoring the effectiveness of the external auditor's performance and their independence and objectivity;		☐	☐	☐	☐	☐	
• developing and implementing a policy on the engagement of the external auditor to supply non-audit services?		☐	☐	☐	☐	☐	

Membership and appointments

	Yes / No / N/A	1	2	3	4	5	Comment
Does the audit committee consist independent non-executive directors?		☐	☐	☐	☐	☐	
Is the board chairman excluded from audit committee membership?		☐	☐	☐	☐	☐	

	Yes / No / N/A	Rating Excellent 1	2	3	Poor 4	5	Comment
Are audit committee members appointed by the board on the recommendation of the nomination committee (where there is one) in consultation with the audit committee chairman?		☐	☐	☐	☐	☐	
Is audit committee membership restricted to a term no longer than three years (extendable by no more than two additional three-year periods)?		☐	☐	☐	☐	☐	

Meetings

	Yes / No / N/A	Rating Excellent 1	2	3	Poor 4	5	Comment
Does the audit committee meet regularly (at least three times a year to coincide with key dates in the financial reporting and audit cycle)?		☐	☐	☐	☐	☐	
Are audit committee meetings well attended?		☐	☐	☐	☐	☐	
Do audit committee meetings allow sufficient time for discussion and questions?		☐	☐	☐	☐	☐	
Are meeting agendas and related background information circulated in a timely manner to enable full and proper consideration to be given to the issues?		☐	☐	☐	☐	☐	
Is sufficient time allowed between audit committee meetings and board meetings to allow any work arising to be carried out and reported to the board as appropriate?		☐	☐	☐	☐	☐	
Does the audit committee invite non-members to attend meetings where necessary? (Only the audit committee members should be entitled to attend audit committee meetings.)		☐	☐	☐	☐	☐	

	Yes / No / N/A	Rating					Comment
		Excellent				Poor	
		1	2	3	4	5	

	Yes / No / N/A	1	2	3	4	5	Comment
Are arrangements in place for the audit committee to meet with external and internal auditors during the year without the presence of management?		☐	☐	☐	☐	☐	
Does the audit committee chairman, and to a lesser extent the other members, keep in touch on a continuing basis with the key people involved in the company's governance, e.g., the board chairman, the chief executive, the finance director, the external auditor and the head of internal audit?		☐	☐	☐	☐	☐	

Training and resources

	Yes / No / N/A	1	2	3	4	5	Comment
Does the audit committee have sufficient skills, experience, time and resources to undertake its duties?		☐	☐	☐	☐	☐	
Does at least one audit committee member have recent and relevant financial experience?		☐	☐	☐	☐	☐	
Is an induction programme (covering the role of the audit committee, its terms of reference and expected time commitment by members; an overview of the company's business; and the main business and financial dynamics and risks) provided for new audit committee members?		☐	☐	☐	☐	☐	
Do audit committee members receive relevant training in financial reporting and related company law on an ongoing and timely basis?		☐	☐	☐	☐	☐	
Do audit committee members have the opportunity to attend formal courses and conferences, internal company talks and seminars, and briefings by external advisers such as the company's auditors and lawyers?		☐	☐	☐	☐	☐	

	Yes / No / N/A	Rating Excellent 1	2	3	Poor 4	5	Comment
Does the audit committee have access to the services of the company secretary and staff?		☐	☐	☐	☐	☐	
Are funds available to enable the audit committee to take independent legal, accounting or other advice when it reasonably believes it necessary to do so?		☐	☐	☐	☐	☐	

Financial reporting

	Yes / No / N/A	Rating Excellent 1	2	3	Poor 4	5	Comment
Does the audit committee review the significant financial reporting issues and judgements made in connection with the preparation of the company's financial statements, interim reports, preliminary announcements and related formal statements?		☐	☐	☐	☐	☐	
Where an accounting treatment is open to a different approach, does the audit committee consider whether the company has adopted appropriate accounting policies and, where necessary, made appropriate estimates and judgements?		☐	☐	☐	☐	☐	
Does the audit committee review the clarity and completeness of disclosures in the financial statements, interim reports, preliminary announcements and related formal statements?		☐	☐	☐	☐	☐	
Where, following its review, the audit committee is not satisfied with any aspect of the proposed financial reporting, does it report such views to the board and seek changes?		☐	☐	☐	☐	☐	

		Rating					
		Excellent				Poor	
	Yes / No / N/A	1	2	3	4	5	Comment

Internal financial controls and risk managements systems

Does the audit committee monitor the integrity of the company's internal financial controls?		☐	☐	☐	☐	☐	
Does the audit committee assist in the boards assessment of the scope and effectiveness of the systems established by management to identify, assess, manage and monitor financial and non financial risks?		☐	☐	☐	☐	☐	
In carrying out such an assessment, does the audit committee receive and review reports from management on the effectiveness of the systems they have established and the results of any testing carried out by internal and external auditors?		☐	☐	☐	☐	☐	
Does the audit committee review and approve the statements included in the annual report in relation to the process for managing risk and the boards review of the adequacy of that process?		☐	☐	☐	☐	☐	

Internal audit process

Where no internal audit function exists, does the audit committee annually consider whether there is a need for one and make a recommendation to the board?		☐	☐	☐	☐	☐	
Does the audit committee review and approve the appointment or termination of the head of internal audit?		☐	☐	☐	☐	☐	
Does the audit committee review and assess the independence and objectivity of the internal audit function?		☐	☐	☐	☐	☐	

	Yes / No / N/A	Rating Excellent 1	2	3	Poor 4	5	Comment
Does the audit committee ensure that the internal auditor has direct access to the board chairman and to the audit committee and is accountable to the audit committee?		☐	☐	☐	☐	☐	
Does the audit committee review and approve the internal audit function's remit?		☐	☐	☐	☐	☐	
Does the audit committee ensure that the internal audit function has the necessary resources and access to information to enable it to fulfil its mandate?		☐	☐	☐	☐	☐	
Does the audit committee review and assess the annual internal audit work plan?		☐	☐	☐	☐	☐	
Does the audit committee receive a report on the results of the internal auditors' work on a periodic basis, and monitor management's responsiveness to the internal auditor's findings and recommendations?		☐	☐	☐	☐	☐	
Does the audit committee meet with the head of internal audit at least once a year without the presence of management?		☐	☐	☐	☐	☐	
Does the audit committee monitor and assess the role and effectiveness of the internal audit function in the overall context of the company's risk management system?		☐	☐	☐	☐	☐	
Does the audit committee make appropriate enquiries about the coordination and cooperation between internal and external audit?		☐	☐	☐	☐	☐	

	Rating						
	Yes / No / N/A	Excellent 1	2	3	4	Poor 5	Comment
Does the audit committee ensure that the internal audit function follows the Standards for the Professional Practice of Internal Auditing issued by the Institute of Internal Auditors?		☐	☐	☐	☐	☐	

External audit process

Is the audit committee responsible for overseeing the external auditor?		☐	☐	☐	☐	☐	
Does the audit committee make recommendations to the board (and thence to shareholders) on the appointment, reappointment and removal of the external auditors?		☐	☐	☐	☐	☐	
Does the audit committee annually assess the qualification, skills and resources, effectiveness and independence of the external auditors?		☐	☐	☐	☐	☐	
Does the audit committee annually assess the procedures in place to ensure the independence and objectivity of the external auditor?		☐	☐	☐	☐	☐	
Does the audit committee seek reassurance that the external auditors and their staff have no family financial, employment, investment or business relationship with the company (other than in the normal course of business)?		☐	☐	☐	☐	☐	
Does the audit committee regularly seek information from the external auditor about its policies and processes for maintaining independence and monitoring compliance with relevant requirements, including current requirements regarding the rotation of audit partners and staff?		☐	☐	☐	☐	☐	

	Yes / No / N/A	Rating					Comment
		Excellent				Poor	
		1	2	3	4	5	
Did the audit committee agree with the board the policy for the employment of former employees of the external auditor, and does the audit committee monitor application of that policy (including the number of former employees of the external auditor currently employed in senior positions in the company)?		☐	☐	☐	☐	☐	
Does the audit committee monitor the external audit firm's compliance with applicable ethical guidance relating to the rotation of audit partners, the level of fees that the company pays in proportion to the overall fee income of the firm, office and partner and other related regulatory requirements?		☐	☐	☐	☐	☐	
Does the audit committee develop and recommend to the board the company's policy in relation to the provision of non-audit services by the auditor?		☐	☐	☐	☐	☐	
Does the audit committee have a policy specifying non-audit work: from which the external auditors are excluded; for which the external auditors can be engaged without referral to the audit committee; and for which a case-by-case decision is necessary?		☐	☐	☐	☐	☐	
Does the audit committee keep the nature and extent of non-audit services provided by the auditors under review?		☐	☐	☐	☐	☐	
Does the audit committee review and agree the engagement letter issued at the start of each audit and, where necessary, ensure that it has been updated to reflect changes in circumstances arising since the previous year?		☐	☐	☐	☐	☐	

	Yes / No / N/A	Rating					Comment
		Excellent				Poor	
		1	2	3	4	5	
Does the audit committee satisfy itself that the level of fee payable in respect of the audit services provided is appropriate and that an effective audit can be conducted for such a fee?		☐	☐	☐	☐	☐	
At the start of each annual audit cycle, does the audit committee consider whether the auditor's overall work plan, including planned levels of materiality, and proposed resources to execute the audit plan appears consistent with the scope of the audit engagement, having regard also to the seniority, expertise and experience of the audit team?		☐	☐	☐	☐	☐	
Does the audit committee: discuss with the external auditor major issues that arose during the course of the audit; review key accounting and audit judgements; review levels of errors identified during the audit, obtaining explanations as to why certain errors might remain unadjusted?		☐	☐	☐	☐	☐	
Does the audit committee review the audit representation letters before signature by management?		☐	☐	☐	☐	☐	
At least annually, does the audit committee meet with the lead audit partner, and other members of the audit team as necessary, without the presence of management, to discuss issues arising from the audit, and any other matters that the auditor might wish to raise with the audit committee and vice versa?		☐	☐	☐	☐	☐	

	Yes / No / N/A	Rating Excellent 1	2	3	Poor 4	5	Comment
As part of the ongoing monitoring process, does the audit committee review the management letter (or equivalent) and monitor management's responsiveness to the external auditor's findings and recommendations?		☐	☐	☐	☐	☐	
At the end of the annual audit cycle, does the audit committee assess the effectiveness of the audit process?		☐	☐	☐	☐	☐	

Whistleblowing

	Yes / No / N/A	1	2	3	4	5	Comment
Does the audit committee review the arrangements by which staff may raise concerns in confidence about possible improprieties in matters of financial reporting, financial control or related matters?		☐	☐	☐	☐	☐	

Relationship with the board

	Yes / No / N/A	1	2	3	4	5	Comment
Does the committee report to the full board after each meeting?		☐	☐	☐	☐	☐	
Where there is disagreement between the audit committee and the board, is adequate time set aside for discussion of the issue with a view to resolving the disagreement?		☐	☐	☐	☐	☐	
Where disagreements between the audit committee and the board cannot be resolved, does the audit committee have the right to report the issue to shareholders?		☐	☐	☐	☐	☐	

		Rating					
		Excellent			Poor		
	Yes / No / N/A	1	2	3	4	5	Comment

Communications with shareholders

Does the audit committee ensure that a report on its role and responsibilities, and the actions taken to discharge those responsibilities is included in the annual report and accounts? Does such a report provide sufficient detail to enable shareholders to understand how the audit committee has discharged its duties?		☐	☐	☐	☐	☐	
Does the report on the audit committee's activities provide sufficient detail to enable shareholders to understand how the audit committee has discharged its duties?		☐	☐	☐	☐	☐	
If the board did not accept the audit committee's recommendation regarding the appointment, reappointment or removal of the auditors, did the audit committee ensure the annual report and accounts included a statement explaining its recommendation and the reasons why the board took a different stance?		☐	☐	☐	☐	☐	
Does the chairman of the audit committee attend the AGM and, where necessary, answer questions on matters within the scope of audit committee's responsibilities?		☐	☐	☐	☐	☐	

Recommendations for improvement

How can the committee improve its performance?

....

....

....

Appendix 5
Example audit committee evaluation of external auditors

The audit committee plays a key role in keeping under review the scope and results of the external audit, its cost effectiveness and the independence and objectivity of the auditors. Where the auditors also supply a substantial volume of non-audit services to the company, the committee should keep the nature and extent of such services under review, seeking to balance the maintenance of objectivity and value for money.

In the current environment, many audit committees are considering how they should discharge their responsibilities in relation to the effectiveness and efficiency of the external audit arrangements. Tendering the audit is by no means the only available option under this responsibility – audit committees are capable of evaluating the performance of their independent auditors and holding them accountable for the performance of their professional duties.

This appendix suggests a checklist framework for an audit committee to carry out a formal review of the effectiveness and efficiency of their external auditors. Such a review provides the audit committee with a disciplined approach to keeping the auditors' performance under review. It will also help to ensure that the auditors remain alert to the company's needs and to maintaining an appropriate relationship with the executive management, the audit committee and the board as a whole.

Calibre of external audit firm

What is the reputation of the external audit firm? Are there recent or current litigation cases against the firm?   ☐

What is the reputation and presence of the external audit firm in this industry?   ☐

Does the external audit firm have the size, resources and geographical coverage required to audit this company?   ☐

Quality processes

What are the quality control processes in the external audit firm?   ☐

Do the factors to be considered include the level and nature of review procedures, the approach to audit judgements and issues, independent quality control reviews and the external audit firms approach to risk?   ☐

How are key audit individuals at the external audit firm compensated and evaluated, and do these compensation and evaluation schemes run the risk of impairing the external auditor's independence? ☐

What is the external audit firm's process for internal review of accounting judgements, including an understanding of the key issues? ☐

What relevant specialists does the external audit firm employ and how are these linked to the audit process? ☐

Audit team

Do the individuals assigned to the external audit team have the requisite expertise, including industry knowledge, to audit this company effectively? ☐

Are sufficient resources allocated to the audit? ☐

What is the scope of the engagement partner's/other senior personnel's involvement in the audit process and is this sufficient? ☐

Does the external audit firm have adequate key team member succession plans in place, which meet the relevant audit partner rotation requirements and facilitate the maintenance of objectivity? ☐

Audit scope

Is the external audit scope adequate to address all of the financial reporting risks facing the company? ☐

Do the factors to be considered include the geographical coverage, the allocated resources, the level of audit testing and the nature of the audit reports issued at each location? ☐

Does the external audit firm agree the audit scope and plan with the audit committee? ☐

Is specialist input to the audit in areas such as taxation, pensions and regulation at an at an appropriate level? ☐

Are all key operations covered by the external audit? ☐

How are overseas audits controlled and is audit effectiveness regarded as consistent internationally? ☐

Are the reporting processes for subsidiary audit teams effective? ☐

What is the external audit firm's approach to seeking and assessing management representations? ☐

Does the external auditor have an effective working relationship with internal audit? ☐

Audit fee

Is the external audit fee reasonable given the scope of the external audit, and how does the audit fee compare with other similarly sized companies in this industry (a fee that is either too high or too low can be of concern)? □

How are differences between actual and estimated fees handled? □

Is an assessment made of the amounts and relationship of audit and non-audit fees and services? □

Audit communications

Does the external audit firm advise the audit committee about significant issues and new developments regarding risk management, corporate governance, financial accounting and related risks and controls on a timely basis? □

Does the external auditor discuss the critical accounting policies and whether the accounting treatment is conservative or aggressive? □

Does the external audit firm meet freely, regularly and on a confidential basis with the audit committee? □

Does the external audit firm resolve accounting issues in a timely manner? □

Does the external audit firm seek feedback on the quality and effectiveness of the service they are providing? □

Audit governance and independence

Is the relationship with the external auditor controlled by the audit committee or does management control the relationship? □

Does the external audit firm have open lines of communication and reporting with the audit committee? □

Are unadjusted audit differences and significant weaknesses in internal controls appropriately communicated? □

Do the individuals assigned to the audit demonstrate a high degree of integrity in their dealings with the audit committee? □

Does the external audit firm discuss their internal process for ensuring independence with the audit committee? □

Does management respect the external auditors as providers of an objective and challenging audit process? □

Is the level and nature of entertainment between the external audit firm and management appropriate? ☐

Does the nature of non-audit services provide any potential to impair audit independence? ☐

Appendix 6
Example audit committee evaluation of internal auditors

The audit committee should evaluate internal audit based on its own experiences and consider asking management and external audit to provide their own assessments. Where the group has subsidiaries or distinct business units, it may be appropriate to make enquiries of the management of such entities. In addition to these assessments, the head of internal audit would generally be expected to self-assess the internal audit department's performance. When the audit committee has studied the answers, other issues may become evident including matters relating to the audit committee's own performance, the performance of management or the performance of external audit.

This appendix provides a four-part checklist of questions to consider as part of a complementary framework for the assessment of the internal audit function that should be completed by the following:

- *Audit committee (initial assessment)*
- *Management*
- *External auditor*
- *Head of internal audit*

The audit committee should ensure they have the appropriate qualified resource to provide answers to these questions and to consider the implications of the findings.

There follows a four-part checklist of questions to consider as part of a complementary framework for the assessment of the internal audit function.

Section A

This part of the checklist should be completed by the audit committee prior to feedback from other areas of the organisation.

Understanding

How well does internal audit demonstrate that it:

- Recognises its direct reporting responsibility to the board of directors and the audit committee;

    Strong ☐ Adequate ☐ Needs improvement ☐

- Has a strong understanding of the responsibilities and operation of the audit committee;

    Strong ☐ Adequate ☐ Needs improvement ☐

- Understands the expectations of the audit committee and the chairman;

  Strong ☐ Adequate ☐ Needs improvement ☐

- Understands the organisation's business and risk environment?

  Strong ☐ Adequate ☐ Needs improvement ☐

Does internal audit consistently demonstrate a realistic and commercial view of the business?

Yes ☐ No ☐

Comments

....

....

....

Charter and structure

Do the terms of reference for internal audit define:

- Roles and responsibilities, including those in relation to other internal functions;

  Yes ☐ No ☐

- Expectations of management;

  Yes ☐ No ☐

- Scope of internal audit work;

  Yes ☐ No ☐

- Access to information?

  Yes ☐ No ☐

Have internal audit's terms of reference been reviewed within the last two years?

Yes ☐ No ☐

Evaluate internal audit's terms of reference in light of the organisation's current needs.

Strong ☐ Adequate ☐ Needs improvement ☐

Evaluate internal audit's current terms of reference in light of the organisation's future needs.

Strong ☐ Adequate ☐ Needs improvement ☐

Are internal audit's terms of reference visible to everyone in the organisation?

Yes ☐ No ☐

Does the structure of internal audit facilitate:

- Consistency in the quality of service to the organisation;

Yes ☐ No ☐

- Understanding of the organisation's business issues;

Yes ☐ No ☐

- The delivering of value to the organisation?

Yes ☐ No ☐

Comments

....

....

....

Skills and experiences

How well does internal audit's staffing reflect it roles and responsibilities?

Strong ☐ Adequate ☐ Needs improvement ☐

On the basis of the work performed by internal audit over the past 12 months, does internal audit appear to have the right staff mix and competencies in specialist areas such as IT and Treasury and the necessary geographical coverage?

Yes ☐ No ☐

Does the internal audit team have an appropriate programme of continuing education?

Yes ☐ No ☐

Evaluate internal audit's independence from the activities it audits.

Strong ☐ Adequate ☐ Needs improvement ☐

How would you assess the committee's confidence in internal audit?

Strong ☐ Adequate ☐ Needs improvement ☐

Comments

....

....

....

Communication

Has internal audit attended all the audit committee meetings it was scheduled to attend?

Yes ☐ No ☐

Has internal audit made itself available for consultation outside of audit committee meetings?

Yes ☐ No ☐

Evaluate internal audit's responsiveness to requests from the audit committee, including requests for special investigations.

Strong ☐ Adequate ☐ Needs improvement ☐

Evaluate internal audit's frankness and candour with the committee.

Strong ☐ Adequate ☐ Needs improvement ☐

Evaluate internal audit's handling of difficult or contentious issues.

Strong ☐ Adequate ☐ Needs improvement ☐

Does internal audit ensure that the chairman of the audit committee is fully briefed on significant findings or developments prior to audit committee meetings?

Yes ☐ No ☐

Evaluate the usual level of preparation for audit committee meetings demonstrated by internal audit.

Strong ☐ Adequate ☐ Needs improvement ☐

Evaluate the quality of internal audit reports and papers tabled with the audit committee. Consider their relevance and clarity.

Strong ☐ Adequate ☐ Needs improvement ☐

Have reports been received from internal audit on a sufficiently timely basis?

Yes ☐ No ☐

Does internal audit promptly advise the audit committee about significant issues and significant developments, including on special projects such as fraud investigations?

Yes ☐ No ☐

Does internal audit promptly advise the committee about significant changes to the internal audit plan?

Yes ☐ No ☐

Evaluate the strength of internal audit's process to monitor the status of open matters/recommendations.

Strong ☐ Adequate ☐ Needs improvement ☐

Did internal audit contribute to the committee's understanding of the overall assurance framework within the organisation and the role internal audit plays in this framework?

Yes ☐ No ☐

Does the internal audit function proactively share its learning widely with the business, i.e. outside the strict reporting channels?

Yes ☐ No ☐

Comments

....

....

....

Performance

This section should include questions that focus on the KPIs for the internal audit team.

Assess the quality of the internal audit plan in terms of its:

- Comprehensiveness, clarity and timeliness;

Strong ☐ Adequate ☐ Needs improvement ☐

- Coverage of priority and high risk areas;

Strong ☐ Adequate ☐ Needs improvement ☐

- Focus on testing the control framework.

Strong ☐ Adequate ☐ Needs improvement ☐

Did the original internal audit plan leave unanswered any significant issues of concern to the audit committee?

Yes ☐ No ☐

What was your assessment of the scope of the internal audit as outlined in the plan?

Strong ☐ Adequate ☐ Needs improvement ☐

Was it clear from its reporting to the committee that internal audit:

- Delivered the services outlined in the plan;

Yes ☐ No ☐

- Was in accordance with the agreed timetable?

Yes ☐ No ☐

Is there evidence of effective coordination of internal and external audit work?

Yes ☐ No ☐

Are success measures used for evaluating the performance of the internal audit function?

Yes ☐ No ☐

Does the internal audit function offer adequate career progression opportunities for its employees?

Yes ☐ No ☐

Are there sufficient performance-based reward mechanisms to motivate internal audit employees?

Yes ☐ No ☐

Do you consider that internal audit has added value to the organisation?

Yes ☐ No ☐

In what way has internal audit added value to the organisation?

....

....

....

How would you assess internal audit's overall performance?

Strong ☐ Adequate ☐ Needs improvement ☐

Overall comments

....

....

....

Name

....

Position: Audit Committee Chairman

....

Signed

....

Date

....

Section B

This part of the checklist should be completed by heads of major business units and the chief financial officer/finance director. Where significant subsidiaries or major business units are subject to internal audit, consider asking leaders of these businesses to complete the survey.

Planning

Are internal audit's terms of reference sufficiently visible to everyone in your business?

Yes ☐ No ☐

Was there sufficient pre-planning and coordination by the internal auditors with the department before each phase of the internal audit or special project commenced?

Yes ☐ No ☐

Did internal audit discuss its approach and major areas of audit focus with you?

Yes ☐ No ☐

Did you raise any major areas of concern that were not reviewed by the internal audit team?

Yes ☐ No ☐

Comments

....

....

....

Skills and experience

Do you consider the internal audit team members have sufficient professional experience, project management, inter-personal skills and seniority to carry out effectively the work required?

Yes ☐ No ☐

Do you consider the internal audit team have sufficient expertise in the functional specialisations (e.g. IT, risk assessment, treasury) to carry out effectively the work that was required?

Yes ☐ No ☐

Assess the strength of internal audit's understanding of the organisation and its risk involvement.

Strong ☐ Adequate ☐ Needs improvement ☐

How strongly did the senior members of the internal audit team demonstrate an appreciation of the issues key to your role and responsibilities?

Strong ☐ Adequate ☐ Needs improvement ☐

Did members of the internal audit team consistently demonstrate independence in all their deliberations?

Yes ☐ No ☐

In your view, does the way in which internal audit is funded impair its independence?

Yes ☐ No ☐

Do you believe the members of the internal audit team are independent of the activities they audit?

Yes ☐ No ☐

Were members of the internal audit team adequately supervised?

Yes ☐ No ☐

Comments

....

....

....

Work programme

Was effective cooperation achieved between the internal auditors and your department, including the avoidance of undue disruption to normal activities?

Yes ☐ No ☐

Was there a formal process to ensure internal audit kept you up to date with audit/project progress?

Yes ☐ No ☐

Did internal audit provide early identification and advice of contentious issues, problem areas and delays?

Yes ☐ No ☐

Did internal audit suggest how such issues could be resolved?

Yes ☐ No ☐

Were suggestions realistic, robust and presented clearly and on a timely basis?

Yes ☐ No ☐

How responsive was internal audit to the business's needs, including requests for special investigations?

Strong ☐ Adequate ☐ Needs improvement ☐

Were internal audit reports:

- Relevant, clear and constructive;

Yes ☐ No ☐

- Sufficiently detailed to enable effective management action;

Yes ☐ No ☐

- Issued on a timely basis?

Yes ☐ No ☐

Were internal audit findings discussed with you prior to being tabled with the audit committee?

Yes ☐ No ☐

Did internal audit follow up recommendations to see whether they had been implemented?

Yes ☐ No ☐

Do you have any major unresolved disagreements with internal audit?

Yes ☐ No ☐

Overall performance

Did internal audit add value to your business?

Yes ☐ No ☐

In what ways did internal audit add value to your business?

....

....

....

Overall comments

....

....

....

Name

....

Position

....

Signed

....

Date

....

Section C

This checklist should be completed by the external auditor of the parent organisation and of subsidiaries, major business units or regions if appropriate.

Terms of reference

Evaluate internal audit's current terms of reference given your understanding of the organisation's business, complexity, risk environment and the current developments in internal audit.

Strong ☐ Adequate ☐ Needs improvement ☐

From your knowledge of internal audit and industry best practice, do you consider internal audit's current terms of reference are maintained at a high quality level?

Yes ☐ No ☐

Comments

....

....

....

Skills and experience

Do you consider the internal audit team members have the professional experience, technical skills, inter-personal skills and seniority to effectively carry out the internal audit work required?

Yes ☐ No ☐

Evaluate the senior members of the internal audit team's understanding of the organisation, its business and its risk environment.

Strong ☐ Adequate ☐ Needs improvement ☐

Assess the internal audit team's experience in key functional specialisations, in the context of what is needed for the proper discharge of their roles and responsibilities:

- IT;

Strong ☐ Adequate ☐ Needs improvement ☐

- Risk management;

Strong ☐ Adequate ☐ Needs improvement ☐

- Treasury;

Strong ☐ Adequate ☐ Needs improvement ☐

- Accounting;

Strong ☐ Adequate ☐ Needs improvement ☐

- Tax;

Strong ☐ Adequate ☐ Needs improvement ☐

- Supply chain.

Strong ☐ Adequate ☐ Needs improvement ☐

Other (specify)

....

....

....

From your dealings with members of the internal audit team and your knowledge of internal audit and industry best practice:

- Do you consider internal audit has sufficient resources to satisfy its terms of reference?

Yes ☐ No ☐

- Evaluate the sufficiency of internal audit's resources to adequately deliver the services outlined in its internal audit plan in the timeframes identified.

Strong ☐ Adequate ☐ Needs improvement ☐

Does the structure of internal audit appear to facilitate understanding of the organisation's business issues?

Yes ☐ No ☐

Does internal audit's staffing appear to reflect adequately its roles and responsibilities?

Yes ☐ No ☐

In your assessment, is the internal audit methodology robust and does it reflect the latest thinking in internal audit?

Yes ☐ No ☐

Comments

....

....

....

Work programme

Are there regular discussions between internal and external audit on internal and external strategies, assessment of risks and the implications of audit findings/audit work?

Yes ☐ No ☐

Has progress against plan been monitored jointly by internal and external audit regularly throughout the year?

Yes ☐ No ☐

Did you receive copies of all internal audit reports issued by internal audit?

Yes ☐ No ☐

Were copies of internal audit reports received on a timely basis?

Yes ☐ No ☐

Are internal audit reports of a standard comparable to best practice in other organisations?

Yes ☐ No ☐

To the best of your knowledge, are there any major areas of risk or concern that internal audit did not appear to cover?

Yes ☐ No ☐

Overall comments

....

....

....

Name

....

Position

....

Signed

....

Date

....

Section D

This checklist should be completed by the head of internal audit (self-assessment).

Understanding

Evaluate internal audit's understanding of:

* The responsibilities and operation of the audit committee;

  Strong ☐ Adequate ☐ Needs improvement ☐

* The organisation's business;

  Strong ☐ Adequate ☐ Needs improvement ☐

* The organisation's risk environment;

  Strong ☐ Adequate ☐ Needs improvement ☐

* The organisation's control framework.

  Strong ☐ Adequate ☐ Needs improvement ☐

Comments

....

....

....

Charter and structure

Do the terms of reference for internal audit define in sufficient detail, for the purposes of directing internal audit:

* Roles and responsibilities, including those in relation to other internal functions;

  Yes ☐ No ☐

- Expectations of management;

Yes ☐ No ☐

- Scope of internal audit work;

Yes ☐ No ☐

- Access to information?

Yes ☐ No ☐

Evaluate internal audit's current terms of reference in light of the organisation's current needs.

Strong ☐ Adequate ☐ Needs improvement ☐

Evaluate internal audit's current terms of reference in light of the organisation's future needs.

Strong ☐ Adequate ☐ Needs improvement ☐

Assess the structure of internal audit in terms of enhancing its:

- Objectivity;

Strong ☐ Adequate ☐ Needs improvement ☐

- Understanding of the organisation's business issues;

Strong ☐ Adequate ☐ Needs improvement ☐

- Ability to respond to business needs.

Strong ☐ Adequate ☐ Needs improvement ☐

Comments

....

....

....

Skills and experience

How well does internal audit's staffing reflect its roles and responsibilities?

Strong ☐ Adequate ☐ Needs improvement ☐

Assess the staff mix and competencies of the internal audit team.

Strong ☐ Adequate ☐ Needs improvement ☐

Evaluate internal audit's independence from the activities it audits.

Strong ☐ Adequate ☐ Needs improvement ☐

Comments

....

....

....

Communication

Evaluate internal audit's responsiveness to requests from the audit committee, including requests for special investigations.

Strong □ Adequate □ Needs improvement □

Evaluate internal audit's frankness and candour with the committee.

Strong □ Adequate □ Needs improvement □

Evaluate internal audit's handling of difficult or contentious issues.

Strong □ Adequate □ Needs improvement □

Over the last 12 months, has the chairman of the audit committee been fully briefed on significant findings or developments prior to audit committee meetings?

Yes □ No □

Evaluate internal audit's process to monitor the status of open matters/recommendations.

Strong □ Adequate □ Needs improvement □

Comments

....

....

....

Performance

This section should be developed to focus on the KPIs set for the internal audit team.

In what way has internal audit added value to the organisation?

....

....

....

How would you assess internal audit's overall performance?

Strong □ Adequate □ Needs improvement □

Overall comments

....

....

....

Name

....

Position

....

Signed

....

Date

....

Appendix 7
Example policy on the use of external auditors for non-audit services

To ensure that non-audit services provided by the auditor do not impair, or appear to impair, the auditor's independence or objectivity, audit committees should develop, and recommend to the board, a policy in relation to the provision of non-audit services. This appendix provides an example of such a policy.

Introduction

This paper sets out the policy for the appointment and remuneration of the external auditors for any work undertaken on behalf of XYZ Plc and outlines the control processes that will be put in place to ensure compliance with this policy.

Statutory audit

The group finance director in conjunction with the relevant member of the group management board will negotiate the annual audit fee for each division and subsidiary. The group finance director will recommend the overall fee for the statutory audit to the group audit committee. It is the responsibility of the audit committee to review the proposed statutory audit fee and recommend it to the XYZ Board for approval.

The audit committee will review the independence and effectiveness of the external auditors on an annual basis.

Other work as auditors or reporting accountants

While it is difficult to be precise regarding the definition of work that the external auditor may undertake as auditor or reporting accountant, it includes the following:
• Interim results and any other review of the accounts for regulatory purposes;
• Assurance work related to compliance and corporate governance, including high level controls;
• Work in connection with listing particulars and prospectuses;
• Regulatory reviews or reviews commissioned by the audit committee; and
• Accounting advice and reviews of accounting standards.

The group chief accountant must clear the appointment of the external auditor for any such work in advance. Any assignments in excess of £x will require the approval of the group finance director, who will consult with the chairman of the audit committee in respect of any assignment over £y.

The audit committee will receive a quarterly report analysing fees paid for other work as auditors or reporting accountants, with additional commentary on assignments agreed during the quarter.

Tax advisory

The external auditor may provide tax advisory services, including tax planning and compliance, provided that such advice does not conflict with the external auditors statutory responsibilities and ethical guidance.

The head of group tax will determine whether the appointment of the external auditor for any tax work would conflict with their statutory duties and, if in any doubt, request approval from the group chief accountant. Any tax assignment in excess of £x requires the approval of the group finance director who will consult with the chairman of the audit committee in respect of any assignment over £y. The audit committee will receive a quarterly report on the tax advisory services provided by the external auditor.

Merger and acquisition support

It is permissible for the external auditor to be appointed to undertake specific activities on behalf of XYZ Plc. However, the external auditor cannot be appointed to undertake merger and acquisition work without the prior approval of the group finance director who will consult with the chairman of the audit committee in respect of any assignment that could involve fees in excess of £x. Any fees paid in respect of merger and acquisition activity will be reported quarterly to the group audit committee.

Other accounting advisory and consultancy work

There may be occasions when the external auditor is best placed to undertake other accounting, advisory and consultancy work on behalf of XYZ Plc due to their in depth knowledge of the company. However, the following are specifically prohibited:
- Work related to accounting records and financial statements that will ultimately be subject to external audit;
- Management of, or significant involvement in, internal audit services;
- Secondments to management positions that involve any decision-making;
- Any work where a mutuality of interest is created that could compromise the independence of the external auditor; and
- Any other work which is prohibited by UK ethical guidance.

Any assignment in excess of £x can only be awarded to the external auditor after competitive tender. The inclusion of the external auditor on a tender list requires the prior approval of the relevant member of the group management board and the group finance director. The group finance director will consult with the chairman of the audit committee regarding any tender for work in excess of £y. Details of all such work and fees paid will be reported quarterly to the group audit committee.

Implementation arrangements

The policy outlined above in respect of new assignments applies with immediate effect. Furthermore, any prohibited secondments from the external auditor should cease by dd/mm/yy at the latest – unless a request for the continuation of the secondment is made to, and agreed by, the chairman of the audit committee.

Appendix 8
Example questions – identifying and assessing risk

In view of the different approaches boards may take in referring powers to the audit committee in respect of risk management and the control framework, it is vital that there is an unambiguous understanding of what the board of directors, other board committees and the audit committee are responsible for in this important area of corporate governance. The audit committee's responsibilities should be reflected in its terms of reference.

So as to meet its responsibilities under its terms of reference, the audit committee needs to assess whether it is getting appropriate risk management information regularly enough and in a format that meets the needs of members. It needs to evaluate at least annually the adequacy and timeliness of management reporting to the committee on financial, non-financial, current and emerging risk trends. The audit committee needs also to discuss risk management with senior executives, internal and external audit. The scope of those discussions should have reference to the audit committee terms of reference.

The following are high-level questions the audit committee may like to consider in framing discussions with management. The list is not exhaustive and will require tailoring based on the audit committee's terms of reference as well as the particular circumstances of the organisation.

Risk management framework	Evaluation of risk management framework
Risk strategy: the approach for associating and managing risks based on the organisation's strategies and objectives.	• What are the risks inherent in our business strategies and objectives? • How is our risk strategy linked to our business strategy? • Is our risk management policy clearly articulated and communicated to the organisation? If not, why not? If yes, how has this been achieved? • Is our risk appetite (the amount of risk the organisation is willing to take) clear? How is it linked to our objectives? • How has the board's perspective on risk permeated the organisation and culture?
Risk structure: the approach for supporting and embedding the risk strategy and accountability.	• Is there a common risk management language/terminology across the organisation? If not, why not? • Is accountability for risk management transparent at the management level? If not, why not? If yes, describe how this has been achieved. • Are risk management activities/responsibilities included in job descriptions? • How do our performance management and incentive systems link to our risk management practices?
Measuring and monitoring: the establishment of KPIs and continuous measuring and improving of performance.	• Are risk owners clearly identified? If not, why not? If yes, how? • Are there systems in place for measuring and monitoring risk? • How are risks, including suspected improprieties, escalated to the appropriate levels within the organisation? • How is the risk management framework linked to the organisation's overall assurance framework?

Risk management framework	Evaluation of risk management framework
Portfolio: the process for identifying, assessing and categorising risks across the organisation.	• Does a comprehensive risk profile exist for the organisation? If not, why not? • Does the risk profile evidence identification and evaluation of non-traditional risk exposures? • Are the interrelationships of risks clearly identified and understood?
	Operational risk • What are the risks inherent in the processes chosen to implement the strategies? • How does the organisation identify, quantify and manage these risks, given its appetite for risk? • How does the organisation adapt its activities as strategies and processes change?
	Reputation risk • What are the risks to brand and reputation inherent in the way the organisation executes its strategies?
	Regulatory or contractual risk • Which financial and non financial risks are related to compliance with regulations or contractual arrangements?
	Financial risk • Have operating processes put financial resources at undue risk? • Has the organisation incurred unreasonable liabilities to support operating processes? • Has the organisation succeeded in meeting measurable business objectives?

Risk management framework	Evaluation of risk management framework
	Information technology risk
	• Is our data/information/knowledge reliable, relevant and timely?
	• Are our information systems reliable?
	• Do our security systems reflect our reliance on technology, including our e-business strategy?
	New risks
	• In a business environment that is constantly changing, are there processes in place to identify emerging risks? If not, why not? If yes, describe them.
	• What risks have yet to develop? These might include risks from new competitors or emerging business models, recession risks, relationship risks, outsourcing risks, political or criminal risks, financial risk disasters such as rogue traders, and other crisis and disaster risks.
Optimisation: balancing potential risks and opportunities based on the appetite to accept risk.	• Does the risk approach include a regular search for new markets, partnering opportunities and other risk optimisation strategies? If not, why not? If yes, how is this achieved?
	• Is risk a priority consideration whenever business processes are improved? If not, why not? If yes, describe how this is achieved.

Appendix 9
Warning signals

Managing risk is about much more than managing the risk of business failure. Nevertheless, the maintenance and regular review of a list of warning signals can be a useful oversight tool. Some warning signals are very company specific, others will be more general. Every organisation is different and each board should develop and maintain its own list of warning signals.

The following are some of the signals audit committee members should be aware of:

1 Financial considerations

- exposure to interest and currency fluctuations;
- organisation's share price has fallen sharply recently;
- overly complex transactions and organisational structures;
- deterioration in the collection of debts and/or quality of debtors;
- increase in amounts owing to creditors;
- ongoing or prior investigations by regulators;
- inadequate information regarding financial performance;
- unusually rapid growth;
- regular deferral of capital expenditure;
- unrealistic earning expectations by financial community;
- explanations for variances from budgets considered to be inadequate;
- excessive or inappropriate performance-based compensation;
- gearing or liquidity forecast to be a problem;
- inadequate review and analysis of budgets against actual performance;
- recognising revenue before sale is complete;
- loan agreement covenants not being complied with;
- results appear unrealistically high given industry and economic conditions;
- key ratios deteriorating;
- significant decline in turnover and market share;
- last minute transactions that result in significant revenues;
- slow-down in the receipt of financial reports;
- financial results consistently meet or closely match budget/forecast;
- unusual results or trends; and
- organisation incurs losses.

2 Board of directors and management

- chairman and chief executive officer dominate meetings and make decisions without first consulting the board;
- autocratic management;

- extremely close relationship between chairman and chief executive officer;
- inappropriate 'tone at the top';
- flow of information delayed, especially concerning problem areas;
- inexperienced management;
- inadequate examination of acquisitions and mergers;
- insufficient questioning and enquiry by board members;
- lack of harmony or respect between board members;
- lack of understanding about technology;
- insufficient number of board committees;
- chief executive officer is a dominant entrepreneur;
- managerial and board self-indulgence;
- lack of management oversight;
- poor relationship between directors and senior management;
- reporting to board only through the chief executive officer;
- board and management focused on the past;
- resignation of key management of directors; and
- failure to comply with code of ethics/conduct.

3 Audit considerations

- auditors' report and management letters show an increasing number of control problems and areas of disagreement with management;
- external auditors changed due to accounting or financial reporting disagreements;
- internal audit operating under restrictions;
- organisation's accounting principles and practices are aggressive or vary from the industry norm;
- untimely reporting and responses to audit committee enquiries; and
- audit committee not meeting with external and internal auditors without management present.

4 Other warning signs

- abnormally high level of related party transactions;
- exposure to rapid technology changes;
- frequent customer complaints about the quality of goods or services provided;
- increasing stock levels compared to turnover;
- major deterioration in any of the organisation's key markets;
- no policy for managing intellectual capital assets;
- insufficient controls over disposal of pollutants;
- performance of major outsourced providers less than adequate;
- insufficient review of compliance with legislative requirements;
- media commenting adversely on the organisation's performance and products;
- deteriorating morale;
- resistance to abandonment of an unprofitable venture;
- not fully understanding overseas market places;

- shortages of raw material or inventories, resulting in the late delivery of orders and indicating a loss of supply markets or late payment of creditors;
- significant drop in sales order activity, especially with forward sales;
- significant staff turnover;
- significant strategic changes in the organisation's operating environment;
- trend of losses appears continuing;
- unexpected losses have occurred;
- major new projects 'out of control' – behind time, significantly over budget, not delivering benefits;
- deteriorating performance on long-term projects;
- consideration of high risk strategies;
- deteriorating relationship with the organisation's banker;
- lack of or inadequate succession planning; and
- bad news not floating to the top.

Appendix 10
ICSA Best Practice Guide: Establishing a Whistleblowing Procedure

Employees are usually the first to become aware of conduct or activities taking place within an organisation which turn out to be cases of serious misconduct or malpractice. Unfortunately, for a number of reasons (such as misplaced loyalty to colleagues or their employer, fear that their concerns will not be taken seriously or that they will be victimised or dismissed) employees with such knowledge often choose not to report their suspicions.

Their silence is not in anyone's interests. The earlier that suspected malpractice is reported, the more quickly it can be investigated and, if proven, dealt with. The State recognises this and, through the Public Interest Disclosure Act 1998, protects against victimisation and dismissal employees who make certain disclosures of information in the public interest. Good practice would be for employers to reflect the principles of the Act in internal procedures that encourage employees to report their legitimate concerns and contain safeguards against misuse.

This guide has been prepared to help employers draw up such procedures.

Commentary on the Public Interest Disclosure Act 1998

The Public Interest Disclosure Act 1998 amends the Employment Rights Act 1996 to give protection from victimisation and dismissal to individuals who make certain disclosures in the public interest.

The Act applies to virtually all employees in the public, private and voluntary sectors, irrespective of their period of employment, and protects them if they make 'qualifying disclosures'. Thus in addition to employees, the Act also covers agency staff, trainees, contractors and home workers. It does not, however, cover the genuinely self-employed (other than in the NHS), volunteers, the intelligence services, the armed forces and the police, and those who normally work overseas.

Qualifying and protected disclosures

In normal circumstances a 'qualifying disclosure' is one which satisfies the three criteria below:
- It is made in good faith;
- It is made in the reasonable belief that the information disclosed tends to reveal one or more of the following:
  - that a criminal offence has been, is being or is likely to be, committed;
  - that there has been, is or is likely to be, a failure to comply with a legal obligation (that is a statutory or contractual requirement, or a common law obligation);
  - that the health or safety of any individual has been, is being or is likely to be endangered;

- that the environment has been, is being or is likely to be damaged;
- that information that shows one of the above has been, is being or is likely to be concealed.

It is made to one of the following:

- the employer (or the person specified by the employer under any internal whistleblowing procedure);
- where the disclosure concerns the actions of a person other than the employer, that person;
- if the disclosure is made in the course of obtaining legal advice, a legal adviser (the requirement for 'good faith' does not apply here);
- in the case of employers of Non Departmental Public Bodies (quangos), the relevant Government Minister; or
- where the worker additionally believes that the allegation and any information contained in the allegation is substantially true, a person or body prescribed by the Secretary of State.

Exceptional circumstances

One of the principles underlying the Act is that those who are accountable for misconduct or malpractice within the workplace should have the opportunity to investigate and deal with it. Thus the provisions of the Act actively encourage organisations to establish formal internal mechanisms for handling reports of malpractice.

However, it is not sufficient for these internal mechanisms simply to exist; they must be robust and effective. If they are not then, in certain circumstances, employees may bypass them and make disclosures to other persons (e.g. the police, non-prescribed regulators or the media). Such an external disclosure will be a 'qualifying disclosure' if it meets the following criteria:

- it is made in good faith;
- it is not made for personal gain;
- in all circumstances it is reasonable for the disclosure to be made; and
- one of the three conditions below is met:
  - the employee reasonably believes that he or she will be victimised by he or she making the disclosure to the employer or the person/body prescribed by the Secretary of State; or
  - the employee has already made the disclosure to his or her employer or the person/body prescribed by the Secretary of State; or
  - there is no prescribed person/body and the employee believes that a disclosure to the employer will result in evidence of suspected malpractice or misconduct being concealed or destroyed.

Employees may also bypass the normal channels if the suspected malpractice or misconduct is exceptionally serious and therefore more appropriately reported to another party, for example the police. Again, however, the disclosure must satisfy the 'good faith', 'personal gain' and 'reasonable in all the circumstances' tests.

Duties of confidentiality and contracts of employment

Although employees owe an implied, and in some cases an express, duty of confidentiality to their employers, the Act specifically invalidates any agreements between employer and employee and any clauses in contracts of employment which would prevent a qualifying disclosure being made.

Employers should also be aware that, where an employee chooses to settle a claim under the Act, it might not be possible to include a non-disclosure clause in that settlement.

Rights of employees

Under the Act, employees who make a qualifying disclosure have the right not to suffer any detriment (such as straightforward dismissal, dismissal under cover of redundancy, bullying, demotion or failure to receive promotion) because of that disclosure. If they do suffer detriment, employees have the right to submit a complaint to an employment tribunal. It is for the tribunal to determine the facts of the case including whether a 'qualifying disclosure' had been made, and any appropriate remedy for the employees.

In deciding whether a 'qualifying disclosure' has been made. The Act provides that an employment tribunal will take into account all the circumstances of a case, including:

- the identity of the person to whom the disclosure was made;
- the seriousness of the malpractice/misconduct;
- whether the malpractice/misconduct is continuing or likely to recur;
- whether the disclosure breaches the employer's duty of confidentiality to a third party;
- whether the disclosure was made in accordance with the employer's internal whistleblowing procedure; and
- the actions that were taken, or might reasonably be expected to have been taken, by the employer (or prescribed person/body) in respect of a previous disclosure.

Essential features of internal whistleblowing procedure

An internal whistleblowing procedure will be effective only if it enjoys the confidence of its intended users: employees. In turn, employees will have confidence in such a policy only if their employer, from the most senior level, is genuinely committed to it. The best way of signalling the employer's commitment and securing employees' confidence is to ensure that the procedure:

- is consistent with other relevant policies and procedures (e.g. contracts of employment, existing disciplinary codes, rules on the provision and acceptance of gifts and hospitality, grievance and internal complaints procedures);
- applies throughout the organisation;
  The 1998 Act applies only to employees normally working in the UK. However, there is a strong case for organisations with overseas employees voluntarily providing those employees with protection equivalent to that enjoyed by their UK counterparts by virtue of the Act.
  Similarly, organisations which make use of the services of the self-employed and volunteers might usefully provide them with protection equivalent to that enjoyed by employees.
- has the support of employees' representatives.

It is essential that employees feel that they are co-owners of a whistleblowing procedure; it should not be seen as something imposed by management. Where possible, employees or their representatives should be actively involved in its drafting and implementation. Consulting with employees in this way will help to identify:

- the issues that are important to the organisation and where in the potential risks of mal-practice lie. It would be sensible to ensure that the policy covers all the types of malpractice defined by the 1998 Act. However, organisations might wish to highlight particular areas: for example fraud and corruption, codes of conduct;
- the factors which may deter staff from raising concerns about such matters and how they may be overcome; and
- key aspects of the whistleblowing arrangements. These will include consideration of whom to designate as being someone to address concerns within the workplace, such as the Company Secretary or the Head of Human Resources.

Ideally, the composition of the consultation group should involve a cross-section of the work-force to reflect accurately the views of staff members. It will also ensure that the whistleblow-ing policy is seen as a genuine attempt to create a more open and responsible working environment. Such a policy:

- Contains a clear statement that the employer takes malpractice/misconduct seriously and is committed to developing an open culture in which staff can report their legitimate con-cerns without fear of penalty.
- Is set out in writing, with copies given to all employees.
- Is publicised in the workplace.
- Gives examples of the kinds of activities/conduct which employees should report by using it.
- Makes it clear that false or malicious allegations will result in disciplinary action.
- Gives details of the persons from whom employees may seek advice on the use of the pro-cedure and related issues.
- Provides both internal and external reporting routes.
- Sets out the procedure by which allegations will be investigated.
- Records allegations and undertakes, as far as is possible, to inform whistleblowers of the outcome of investigations.
- Maintains, as far as is possible, confidentiality for whistleblowers where this is requested.
- Makes provision for monitoring the use and effectiveness of the policy.

Model internal whistleblowing procedure

Our assurances to you

The Board and Chief Executive of [Organisation name] are committed to maintaining the highest standards of honesty, openness and accountability and recognises that you have an important role to play in achieving this goal.

Employees will usually be the first to know when someone inside or connected with an organ-isation is doing something illegal or improper, but often they feel apprehensive about voicing their concerns. This may be because they feel that speaking up would be disloyal to their colleagues or the organisation itself. Or it may be because they do not think that their concerns will be taken seriously because, they are afraid that they will be bullied or dismissed. However, [Organisation name] does not believe that it is in anyone's interests for employees with knowledge of wrongdoing to remain silent.

[Organisation name] takes all malpractice very seriously, whether it is committed by senior managers, staff, suppliers or contractors; this document sets out a procedure by which you can report your concerns to us.

This procedure has been [drawn up in consultation with/endorsed by] [name of trade union/employees' representatives].

What sort of activities should I report using this procedure?

It is impossible to give an exhaustive list of the activities that constitute misconduct or malpractice but, broadly speaking, [organisation name] would expect you to report the following:

- Criminal offences;
- Failure to comply with legal obligations;
- Miscarriages of justice;
- Actions which endanger the health or safety of staff or the public;
- Actions which cause damage to the environment; and
- Actions which are intended to conceal any of the above.

It will not always be clear that a particular action falls within one of these categories and you will need to use your own judgement. However, [organisation name] would prefer you to report your concerns rather than keep them to yourself. If you make a report in good faith then, even if it is not confirmed by an investigation, your concern will be valued and appreciated and you will not be liable to disciplinary action. However, if you make a false report, maliciously or for personal gain, then you may face disciplinary action.

How do I make a report?

You can make a report orally or in writing. [Organisation name] would normally expect you to raise your concerns internally to either:

- your line manager (or his or her superior); or
- [designated senior manager].

Which of these individuals is the more appropriate will depend on the serious of the malpractice and who you think is involved in it. If, under the circumstances, you do not feel comfortable about making a report directly to management, then you can report instead to:

- [name and contact details of designated 'independent' person].

Please say if you want to raise the matter in confidence so that appropriate arrangements can be made.

Independent advice

If you are unsure whether to use this procedure or you want independent advice at any stage, you may contact the independent charity Public Concern at Work on (020) 7404 6609.

External contacts

While we hope that this policy gives you the reassurance you need to raise such matters internally, [organisation name] recognises that there may be circumstances (for example, where the wrongdoing is extremely serious) where it may be appropriate for you to report your concerns to an outside body, such as the police. Public Concern at Work will be able to advise you on such an option and the circumstances in which you may be able to contact an outside body safely.

Do I need proof of wrongdoing to make my report?

[Organisation name] does not expect you to have absolute proof of any misconduct or malpractice that you report. However, you will need to be able to show the reasons for your concern.

Will [Organisation name] protect my identity if I make a report?

[Organisation name] will do everything possible to keep your identity secret, if you so wish. However, there may be circumstances (for example, if your report becomes the subject of a criminal investigation) wherein you may be needed as a witness. Should this be the case we will discuss the matter with you at the earliest opportunity.

How will my report be investigated?

Once you have made a report [Organisation name] will acknowledge receipt of it within [5] working days.

There are, of course, two sides to every story and [organisation name] will need to make preliminary enquiries to decide whether a full investigation is necessary. If such an investigation is necessary then, depending on the nature of the misconduct, your concerns will be either:

- investigated internally (by management, internal audit, personnel); or
- referred to the appropriate external person (for example our external auditors or the police) for investigation.

Subject to any legal constraints, [Organisation name] will inform you of the outcome of the preliminary enquiries, full investigation and any further action that has been taken.

What can I do if I am unhappy with the way [Organisation name] has dealt with my report?

If you are unhappy with the outcome of an investigation, [Organisation name] would prefer that you submit another report explaining why this is the case. Your concern will be investigated again if there is good reason to do so.

However, it may be that you do not think that this is appropriate and wish to raise your concern with an external organisation, such as a regulator. It is, of course, open for you to do so provided you have sufficient evidence to support your concern.

[Organisation name] strongly advises that before reporting your concern externally, you seek advice from one of the following:

- [Contact details of employees' representatives];
- Public Concern at Work
  Suite 306
  16 Baldwin's Gardens
  London EC1N 7RJ
  Tel: (020) 7404 6609

While [Organisation name] cannot guarantee that we will respond to your report in the way that you might wish, we will try to handle the matter fairly and properly. By using this procedure, you will help us to achieve this.

About 'Public Concern at Work'

Public Concern at Work is an independent charity which promotes good practice, compliance with the law and accountability in the workplace.

Public Concern at Work is recognised as a leader in its field and its work has been endorsed by Government, the Committee on Standards in Public Life, the TUC, the CBI and the Institute of Directors. Among the services it provides to organisations in the public, private and voluntary sectors are:

- A helpline staffed by qualified lawyers providing advice, free of charge, to employees.
- A consultancy service assisting clients in developing and implementing effective whistle-blowing policies.
- A Policy Pack for employers.

Public Concern at Work can be contacted at:

Suite 306
Baldwins Gardens
London EC1N 7RJ.
Tel: 020 7404 6609.
Fax: 020 7404 6576.
e-mail: whistle@pcaw.demon.co.uk

Appendix 11
Example policy on the employment of former employees of the external auditor

The audit committee should agree a policy for the employment of former employees of the external auditor, taking into account the relevant ethical guidelines governing the accounting profession. Particular attention should be paid to those individuals who were part of the audit team and moved directly to the company. This appendix contains an example policy on the employment of former employees of the external auditor.

The audit committee has adopted the following policy regarding the employment of former employees of the company's external auditor.

For purposes of this policy, the 'audit team' means any partner, director, manager, staff, reviewing actuary or reviewing tax professional associated with the company's external auditor who works on any aspect of the annual audit of the company's consolidated financial statements. For purposes of this policy, 'employee of the company's independent auditing firm' will include any person regularly providing professional services on behalf of the independent auditor, regardless of whether that person is legally an employee of the firm – for example, if the external auditor is a partnership, a partner would be deemed an 'employee of the company's independent auditor'. For purposes of these guidelines, 'company' includes XYZ Plc and its subsidiaries.

- No member of the audit team can be hired into in a financial reporting oversight role, for a period of two years following their association with the audit. A financial oversight role is any position that has direct responsibility for overseeing those who prepare the company's financial statements.
- No former employee of the company's external auditor may be named a company officer for two years after the termination of their employment with the company's external auditor.
- No former employee of the company's external auditor may join the senior executive team without the approval of the human resources director and the chairman of the audit committee.
- Each year, the human resources director shall report to the audit committee the profile of former employees of the external auditor employed by the company in the preceding year.

Appendix 12
Example audit committee disclosures

Compliance with the Combined Code requires that a separate section of the annual report should describe the role and responsibilities of the audit committee and how it has discharged those duties. Specimen audit committee disclosures are provided in this appendix.

Audit committee

The audit committee consists of four non-executive directors, considered by the board to be independent. These are [ ] (chairman), [ ], [ ] and [ ]. The committee has at least one member possessing what the Smith Guidance describes as recent and relevant financial experience. [ ], a chartered accountant, was finance director of [ ] between 1998 and 2002. It will be seen from the directors' biographical details, appearing on pages XX and XX, that the other members of the committee bring to it a wide range of experience from positions at the highest level both in the UK and the rest of the world.

The committee normally meets four times a year and did so during the year under review.

Both the external auditors and the internal auditor are present at the meetings and, in addition, it is common practice for the committee to meet the external auditors without management present as part of each meeting. There are no members of management on the committee. The chief executive officer, the finance director and other members of management attend audit committee meetings at the invitation of the audit committee chairman.

The main role and responsibilities are set out in written terms of reference which are available for inspection on the company's website and include:

- monitoring the integrity of the company's financial statements and reviewing significant financial reporting issues and judgments contained therein;
- reviewing the company's systems of financial control and risk management;
- monitoring and reviewing the effectiveness of the company's internal audit function;
- making recommendations to the board on the appointment and dismissal of the external auditor and approving their remuneration and terms of engagement; and
- monitoring and reviewing the external auditors' independence, objectivity and effectiveness, taking into account professional and regulatory requirements.

These responsibilities are discharged as follows:

- At its meetings in February and August, the audit committee reviews of the company's preliminary announcement/annual report and accounts, and the interim report respectively. On both occasions, the committee receives reports from the external auditors identifying any accounting or judgmental issues requiring its attention.

- A quarterly report from the head of internal audit is presented at each of the four meetings. In addition, at the November meeting, the head of internal audit submits the department's audit plans for the coming year.
- The external auditors also present their audit plans at the November meeting and, at the May meeting, there is a detailed review of the management letter covering the auditors' findings in respect of the prior financial year.
- Executives are, from time to time, required to make presentations to the audit committee on the subject of risk, its identification, management and control.
- As a matter of routine, the audit committee is presented with information on material litigation involving the company.

As noted above, one of the duties of the audit committee is to make recommendations to the board in relation to the appointment of the external auditors. A number of factors are taken into account by the committee in assessing whether to recommend the auditors for re-appointment. These include:

- the quality of reports provided to the audit committee and the board and the quality of advice given;
- the level of understanding demonstrated of the company's business and industry; and
- the objectivity of the auditors' views on the controls around the company and their ability to coordinate a global audit working to tight deadlines.

The audit committee has put in place safeguards to ensure that the independence of the audit is not compromised. Such safeguards include:

- seeking confirmation that the auditors are, in their professional judgement, independent of the company;
- obtaining from the external auditors an account of all relationships between the auditors and the company;
- monitoring the number of former employees of the external auditors currently employed in senior positions in the company and assessing whether those appointments impair, or appear to impair, the auditors' judgement or independence;
- considering whether, taken as a whole, the various relationships between the company and the external auditors impairs, or appears to impair the auditors' judgement or independence;
- considering whether the compensation of individuals employed by the external auditors who are performing the audit is tied to the provision of non-audit services and, if so, consider whether this impairs, or appears to impair, the external auditors' judgement or independence; and
- reviewing the economic importance of the company to the external auditors and assessing whether that importance impairs, or appears to impair, the external auditors' judgement or independence.

The company has a policy governing the conduct of non-audit work by the auditors. Under that policy the auditors are prohibited from performing services where the auditors:

- may be required to audit their own work;
- participate in activities that would normally be undertaken by management;

- are remunerated through a 'success fee' structure, where success is dependent on the audit; and
- act in an advocacy role for the company.

Other than the above, the company does not impose an automatic ban on the company's auditor undertaking non-audit work. The auditor is permitted to provide non-audit services that are not, or are not perceived to be, in conflict with auditor independence, providing they have the skill, competence and integrity to carry out the work in the best interests of the company. A list of these types of services is contained in company's policy which can be found on the company's website. All services that fall into this category where fees are in excess of £x, must be approved by the audit committee. Activities that may be perceived to be in conflict with the role of the external auditor must be submitted to the committee for approval prior to engagement, regardless of the amounts involved. All assignments are monitored by the committee.

Details of the amounts paid to the external auditors during the year for audit and other services are set out in the notes to the financial statements on page XX.

Appendix 13
Example internal audit plan

Where an internal audit function exists, the audit committee should be involved in developing and approving the internal audit department's mandate, goals and mission. The internal audit work plan should be reviewed, in collaboration with management, to ensure it covers the right areas – a proper balance between the assessment of internal controls related to financial reporting and other special projects, operational efficiency and risk management responsibilities. A specimen internal audit plan is included in this appendix.

Internal audit work by division:

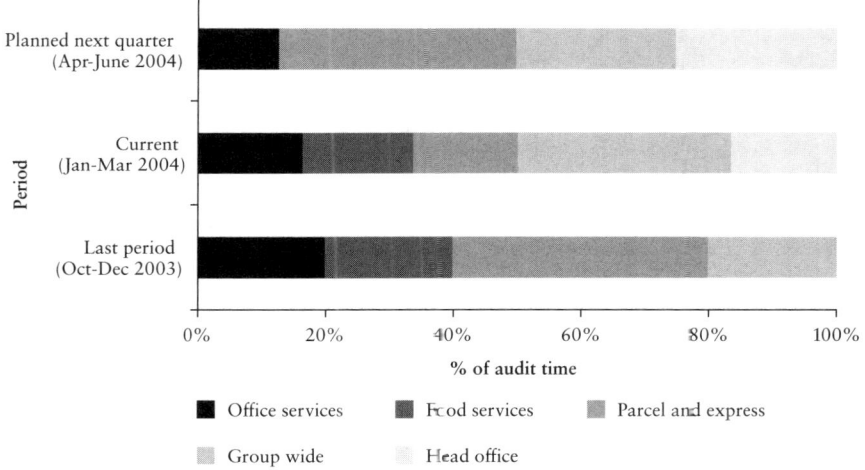

The internal audit plan to be carried out between April and June 2004 is as follows:

Review	Scope	Location	Timetable
Review of procedures to monitor bank covenants	• Head office review of monitoring processes and procedures • Integrity audit of reported key performance indicators • Review of documentation used by Group Finance to communicate requirements of UK GAAP and monitor compliance	London	April 2004 1 week
Review of contract accounting and revenue recognition in Office Services Division	• Review of proposed Contract Controls Framework	Office Services Division	May 2004 2 weeks
Extension of scope of post-implementation review of Sales Order Processing and Customer Database systems	• Review of Readiness Review checklist • Review of project management procedures	European Operations	June 2004 3 weeks
Review of processes to monitor performance of sub-contractors	• Benchmarking with industry best practice of key performance indicators used to measure and monitor performance • Review of integrity of key performance indicators • Review of management monitoring procedures	Germany	June 2004 2 weeks

Review	Scope	Location	Timetable
Review of copyright procedures	• Review of project planning, design and implementation process documentation to ensure compliance with copyright legislation	Germany	April 2004 2 weeks
Monthly review of operation of key financial controls within Finance Departments	• Using self assessment internal financial controls questionnaire, validate existence and operation of key financial controls	All Finance Departments	Ongoing and monthly 2 days each month per country
Review of vetting procedures for temporary staff	• Review procedures to ensure that temporary staff are vetted prior to engagement • Review the updated policy documentation • Review the proposed guidelines on restrictions to be placed on the role and responsibilities of temporary staff	Group Finance/Human Resources	May 2004 2 days

Appendix 14
Example risk summary and register

Audit committees should determine that management has implemented policies that ensure the company's risks around financial reporting (and, where applicable, the wider sphere of business risk) are identified and that controls are adequate, in place, and functioning properly. As part of its assessment, the audit committee should consider requesting from management an overview of the risks, policies, procedures, and controls in order for it to gain meaningful insight into the key sources of risk and how such risks are managed. An example risk summary, designed to give audit committee members a quick insight into the key risks and the effectiveness of the controls in place, is included below.

Significant progress has been made in the development and implementation of the group's risk management policy. The process is to identify, assess and manage the group's key risks, to support the business objectives. The output from the risk management process is now used as a tool to manage the group on an ongoing basis, rather than being seen as a stand alone exercise for the Annual Report. The purpose of this section of our report is to present management's view of the top 10 key risks facing the business. Each of these risks has been assessed in terms of potential impact and likelihood of occurrence, using descriptive scales. Quantification criteria for likelihood and impact is set below the risk summary.

The grid opposite has been used to provide a graphical illustration of the likelihood and impact for each of the group's top ten risks, the arrows representing the influence existing internal controls are thought to have on that risk. (Refer to pages 121 to 126 for the summary risk register.)

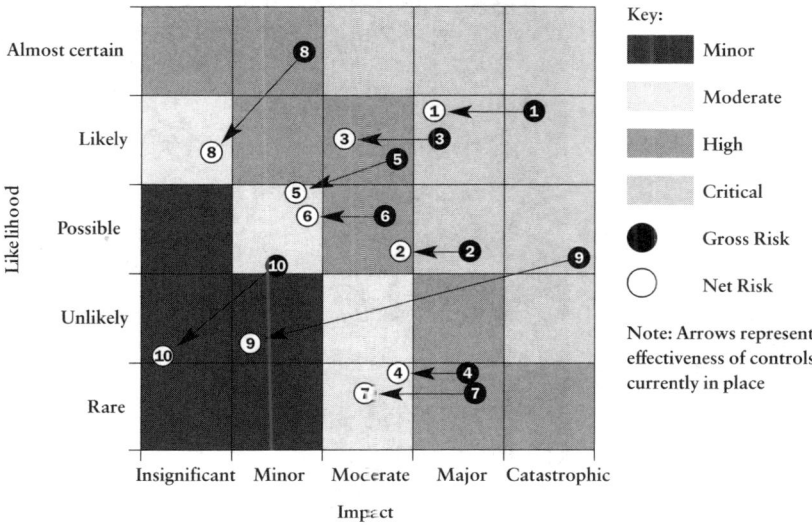

Top ten key risks:

1) Inappropriate acquisition strategy and process

2) Fall in investor confidence due to media criticism

3) Failure to comply with appropriate regulatory and legal requirements (i.e., cartels)

4) Post implementation IT systems failures

5) Failure to allow current business strategy enough time to develop

6) Failure to manage and respond adequately to economic uncertainty

7) Inadequate business continuity and disaster recovery plans to manage a major IT network failure

8) Inability to protect brand name

9) Parcel and express services division fail to deliver their expected growth strategy

10) Loss of key staff and inadequate succession planning.

Quantification criteria for likelihood and impact

Likelihood			
Almost certain	5	>90%	Event is expected to occur in most circumstances
Likely	4	50–90%	Event will probably occur in most circumstances
Possible	3	30–50%	Event should occur at some time
Unlikely	2	10–30%	Event could occur at some time
Rare	1	<10%	Event may occur only in exceptional circumstances

	1 Insignificant	2 Minor	3 Moderate	4 Major	5 Catastrophic
Time	Resolution would be achieved during normal day to day activity	Resolution would require input from regional management team	Resolution would require input from Executive team	Resolution would require the mobilisation of a dedicated project team	Resolution would require input from the Board
Profit	Less than 1% or no impact	1% to 3% impact	3% to 10% impact	10% to 25% impact	Greater than 25%

Key:

- Minor
- Moderate
- High
- Critical

Turnover	Little or no impact	1% to 3% impact	3% to 10% impact	10% to 25% impact	Greater than 25%
Environment	On-site environmental exposure immediately contained	On-site environmental exposure contained after prolonged effort	On-site environmental exposure contained with outside assistance	Off-site environmental exposure contained with outside assistance	Environmental exposure off-site with detrimental effects
Reputation	Letters to local/industry press	Series of articles in local/industry press	Extended negative local/industry media coverage	Short term national negative media coverage	Extensive negative national media coverage
Regulatory	Minor breaches by individual staff members	No fine – no disruption to scheduled services	Fine but no disruption to scheduled services	Fine and disruption to scheduled services	Significant disruption to scheduled services over an extended period of time
Management effort	An event, the impact of which can be absorbed through normal activity	An event, the consequences of which can be absorbed but management effort is required to minimise the impact	A significant event which can be managed under normal circumstances	A critical event which with proper management can be endured	A disaster with potential to lead to collapse of the business

Impact

Summary Risk Register

Risk	Gross risk Impact	Gross risk Likelihood	Board accountability	Control description	Control effectiveness	Net/residual risk Impact	Net/residual risk Likelihood	Action	Responsibility	Review date
1 Inappropriate acquisition strategy and process	5	4	Finance Director	Use of external advisors for due diligence	Weak	4	4	Develop mergers and acquisitions framework aligned with business strategy. Widening of acquisition. search function.	Finance Director	Sept 2004
2 Fall in investor confidence due to media criticism	4	3	Chief Executive	Annual meeting with key investors	Poor	3	3	Media training for all executives. Open days. Formal and informal programme of contacts.	Head of Communications	June 2004

Risk	Gross risk Impact	Gross risk Likelihood	Board accountability	Control description	Control effectiveness	Net/residual risk Impact	Net/residual risk Likelihood	Action	Respons-ibility	Review date
3 Failure to comply with appropriate regulatory and legal requirements (i.e., cartels).	4	4	Entire Board	Yearly self-assessment. Oversight by Legal department.	Poor	3	4	Health check on all procedures regarding regulatory and legal compliance.	Head of Legal	June 2004
4 Post imple-mentation IT systems failures.	4	2	Finance Director	Project management procedures, Utilisation of Readiness Review checklist on all projects.	Good	3	2	Maintenance of offsite back-ups.	Head of IT	June 2004
5 Failure to allow current business strategy enough time to develop.	3	4	Entire Board	Board's continuous review of group strategy.	Good	2	3	Setting of strong KPIs for business strategy and realistic review dates.	Chief Executive	June 2004

Risk	Gross risk		Board accountability	Control description	Control effectiveness	Net/residual risk		Action	Responsibility	Review date
	Impact	Likelihood				Impact	Likelihood			
6 Failure to manage and respond adequately to economic uncertainty.	3	3	Chief Executive, Finance Director, Division MDs	Management monthly review of economic forecast and comparison with the group's forecast financial position.	Good	2	3	Creation of financial models in order to conduct scenario modelling.	Board	Sept 2004
7 Inadequate business continuity and disaster recovery plans to manage a major IT network failure.	4	1	Finance Director	Business continuity and disaster recovery plans reviewed (and update where necessary) and tested half-yearly.	Strong	3	1	Off site back-up of systems.	Head of IT	Sept 2004

Risk	Gross risk		Board accountability	Control description	Control effectiveness	Net/residual risk		Action	Responsibility	Review date
	Impact	Likelihood				Impact	Likelihood			
8 Inability to protect brand name.	2	5	Chief Executive, Finance Director	Copyright procedures in place. Quarterly management review process to ensure compliance with copyright legislation. Legal review of all copyrights.	Good	1	4	Review and update (if necessary) copyright procedures.	Head of Legal	Sept 2004
9 Parcel and Express services division fail to deliver their expected growth strategy.	5	3	Chief Executive, MD Parcel and Express Services	Growth strategy devised following regional consultation with senior management.	Good	2	2	Regular review of strategy and performance against KPIs in management meetings.	MD Parcel & Express services	June 2004

Risk	Gross risk		Board accountability	Control description	Control effectiveness	Net/residual risk		Action	Responsibility	Review date
	Impact	Likelihood				Impact	Likelihood			
				Good KPI framework with regular monitoring. Widespread communication of strategy.						
10 Loss of key staff and inadequate succession planning.	2	3	Chief Executive, Division MDs	Salary review. Well defined succession planning for key members. Well defined recruitment processes. Strong recruitment processes.	Strong	1	2	Annual benchmarking of salaries compared to industry peer group.	Head of Human Resources	Sept 2004

Appendix 15
Comparison of the Smith Guidance to relevant SEC and NYSE regulations

This appendix sets out a summary comparison of Sir Robert Smith's Guidance on Audit Committees *(as appended to the revised Combined Code issued in July 2003) and selected elements of SEC and NYSE audit committee related regulation. This summary is meant to provide a high-level overview of elements of the new requirements that impact audit committees.*

This document does not incorporate all of the elements of these requirements, nor does it consider regulations that may have previously existed (such as the stock exchange listing standards and SEC regulations issued in December 1999). Audit committees should consult with legal counsel in the application the stock exchange listing requirements to specific situations.

	Smith Guidance for Audit Committees	NYSE Audit Committee Regulations	SEC Audit Committee Regulations
Applicability	The Smith Guidance is designed to suggest ways of applying the relevant principles and of complying with the relevant provisions of the revised Combined Code. The rules of the UK Listing Authority require UK listed companies to state the extent to which they have complied with the provisions contained within the Combined Code (exemptions exist for companies that have only debt securities, or fixed income shares listed).	The new NYSE listing standards apply to companies listing common equity securities. Controlled companies, limited partnerships and companies in bankruptcy, closed-end and open-end funds, foreign private issuers and some other specified entities are exempt from specific provisions in the standards. The standards apply to companies that list only debt or preferred securities only to the extent that the listing standards overlap with SEC Rule 10A-3 and for purposes of CEO notifications of known material non-compliance with the listing rules.	The final SEC rules on audit committees apply to all listed issuers.
Compliance date	Applies to accounting periods beginning on or after 1 November 2003.	Generally, US listed companies must comply by the date of their first shareholder's meeting after 15 January 2004, but in any event no later then 31 October 2004. Foreign-private issuers are required to comply no later than 31 July 2005.	Foreign private issuers are be required to comply by the date of their first annual shareholders meetings after 31 July 2005. US listed issuers are required to comply by the date of their first annual shareholder's meeting after 15 January 2004, but in any event no later then 31 October 2004.

	Smith Guidance for Audit Committees	NYSE Audit Committee Regulations	SEC Audit Committee Regulations
Conse-quences of non-compliance	The 'comply or explain' principle of the Combined Code applies. Departures from the Combined Code and related Smith Guidance will not be automatically treated as breaches.	Violation of the Corporate Responsibility criteria including the rules on audit committees could result in de-listing.	Companies will be de-listed if they fail to implement SEC regulations, and do not successfully cure violations.
Purpose	The main role and responsibilities of audit committees should be set out in written terms of reference and should include: • to monitor the integrity of the financial statements of the company and any formal announcements relating to the company's financial performance, and reviewing significant financial reporting judgements contained in them; • to review the company's internal financial control system and, unless addressed by a separate risk committee or by the board itself, risk management systems; • to monitor and review the effectiveness of the company's internal audit function;	The purpose of the audit committee is to assist the board of directors in the oversight of the: • integrity of financial statements; • company's compliance with legal and regulatory requirements; • external auditor's qualifications and independence; and • performance of company's internal audit function and external auditors. The audit committee must also prepare the report required by SEC rules to be included in annual proxy statement (report to shareholders).	The purpose of the audit committee is to assist the board of directors in the oversight of: • accounting and financial reporting processes; • the effectiveness of financial reporting controls; and • the independence, accountability and effectiveness of the external auditor.

Smith Guidance for Audit Committees	NYSE Audit Committee Regulations	SEC Audit Committee Regulations
• to make recommendations to the board in relation to the appointment of the external auditor and to approve the remuneration and terms of engagement of the external auditor following appointment by the shareholders in General Meeting; • to review and monitor the external auditor's independence and objectivity and the effectiveness of the audit process; and • to develop and implement policy on the engagement of the external auditor to supply non-audit services.		
Membership The board should establish an audit committee of at least three or, in the case of companies outside the FTSE 350, two members. Audit committees should be comprised solely of independent non-executive directors.	The board should establish an audit committee of at least three members, all of whom are independent directors.	Each member of the audit committee must be independent, one member must be a financial expert (defined below).

Smith Guidance for Audit Committees	NYSE Audit Committee Regulations	SEC Audit Committee Regulations
An 'independent' director is one who is independent in character and judgement and has no relationships or circumstances that affect his or her judgement. Such relationships and circumstances would include where the director was an employee within the last five years, where the director holds cross directorships or has significant links with other directors through involvement in other company boards or bodies, and where the director has served on the board for more than nine years. The chairman of the company should not be an audit committee member.	No director qualifies as 'independent' unless the board of directors affirmatively determines that the director has no material relationship with the listed company (either directly or as a partner, shareholder or officer of an organisation that has a relationship with the company). Companies must disclose these determinations. The rules include a number of other detailed provisions relating to previous employment and related remuneration levels.	There are two basic criteria for audit committee member independence: • audit committee members must be barred from accepting any consulting, advisory or compensatory fee from the issuer or any subsidiary, other than in the member's capacity of the board or any board committee; and • an audit committee member must not be an affiliated person of the issuer or any subsidiary of the issuer.
At least one member of the audit committee should have recent and relevant financial experience.	All members must be financially literate or must become financially literate within a reasonable period of time after becoming audit committee members. At least one member must have expertise in accounting or related financial management.	The SEC has defined an audit committee financial expert as a person who has all of the following attributes: • an understanding of generally accepted accounting principles and financial statements;

Smith Guidance for Audit Committees	NYSE Audit Committee Regulations	SEC Audit Committee Regulations
	A board may presume that a person who meets the SEC's definition of an 'audit committee financial expert' [see SEC column for definition] has the accounting or related financial management expertise required under the new listing standards.	• the ability to assess the general application of such principles in accounting for estimates, accruals and reserves; • an understanding on internal controls and procedures for financial reporting; • an understanding of internal controls and procedures for financial reporting; • experience preparing, auditing, analysing or evaluating financial statements that present a breadth and level of complexity of accounting issues that are generally comparable to the breadth and complexity of issues that can be reasonably be expected to be raised; and • an understanding of audit committee functions.

Smith Guidance for Audit Committees	NYSE Audit Committee Regulations	SEC Audit Committee Regulations
The need for a degree of financial literacy among the other members will vary according to the nature of the company, but experience of corporate financial matters will normally be required.		The SEC requires disclosure of whether the audit committee has at least one financial expert. If an audit committee does not have a financial expert the reason why must be disclosed.
	If the audit committee does not have a member who meets the SEC's definition of an 'audit committee financial expert' that fact must be disclosed, even if the NYSE listing requirement is met.	

	Smith Guidance for Audit Committees	NYSE Audit Committee Regulations	SEC Audit Committee Regulations
Meetings	Only audit committee members should be entitled to be present at audit committee meetings. Others may be invited to attend. The audit committee should, at least annually, meet the external and internal auditors, without management, to discuss issues arising from the audit. A sufficient interval should be allowed between audit committee meetings and	The audit committee should meet separately on a periodic basis with management, internal auditors and the external auditors.	

	Smith Guidance for Audit Committees	NYSE Audit Committee Regulations	SEC Audit Committee Regulations
	main board meetings to allow any work arising from the audit committee meeting to be carried out and reported to the board as appropriate.		
Resources	The audit committee should be provided with sufficient resources to undertake its duties.	The audit committee shall have authority and funding to engage independent counsel and outside advisors as appropriate without seeking approval of the board of directors.	Audit committees should be provided with funding to fulfil their responsibilities. This includes money to pay the independent auditor and hire outside advisors.
Pay	In addition to the remuneration paid to all non-executive directors, each company should consider the further remuneration that should be paid to members of the audit committee to recompense them for the additional responsibilities of membership. Consideration should be given to the following: • the time members are required to give to audit committee business; • the skills they bring to bear and the onerous duties they take on; and		Audit committee members may not accept either directly or indirectly any consulting, advisory or compensatory fees from the issuer or any subsidiary other than the fees related to service on the board of directors or any board committee.

Smith Guidance for Audit Committees	NYSE Audit Committee Regulations	SEC Audit Committee Regulations
• the value of their work to the company. The level of remuneration paid to the members of the audit committee should take into account the level of fees paid to other members of the board. The chairman's responsibilities and time demands will generally be heavier than the other members of the audit committee and this should be reflected in his or her remuneration.		
Training An induction programme should be provided for new audit committee members. This should cover: • the role of the audit committee, including its terms of reference and expected time commitment by members; and • an overview of the company's business, identifying the main business and financial dynamics and risks. Meeting some of the company staff is also recommended.	The company's corporate governance guidelines must address director orientation and continuing education.	

Smith Guidance for Audit Committees	NYSE Audit Committee Regulations	SEC Audit Committee Regulations
Training should also be provided to members of the audit committee on an ongoing and timely basis and should, at least, include an understanding of the principles of, and developments in, financial reporting and related company law. In appropriate cases, it may also include: • understanding financial statements, applicable accounting standards and recommended practice; • the regulatory framework for the company's business; and • the role of internal and external auditing and risk management. The induction programme and ongoing training may take various forms, including attendance at formal courses and conferences, internal company talks and seminars, and briefings by external advisers.		

	Smith Guidance for Audit Committees	NYSE Audit Committee Regulations	SEC Audit Committee Regulations
Relationship with the board	Nothing in the guidance should be interpreted as a departure from the principle of the unitary board. All directors remain equally responsible for the company's affairs as a matter of law. The audit committee, like other committees to which particular responsibilities are delegated (such as the remuneration committee), remains a committee of the board. Any disagreement within the board, including disagreement between the audit committee's members and the rest of the board, should be resolved at board level. The role of the audit committee is for the board to decide and to the extent that the audit committee undertakes tasks on behalf of the board, the results should be reported to, and considered by, the board.	The audit committee should report regularly to the board of directors any issues concerning: • quality and integrity of financial statements; • compliance with legal or regulatory requirements; • performance and independence of the external auditors; and • performance of internal audit function. The audit committee should present its conclusions with respect to the qualifications, performance and independence of the external auditors to the full board.	

	Smith Guidance for Audit Committees	NYSE Audit Committee Regulations	SEC Audit Committee Regulations
	The terms of reference of the audit committee should be tailored to the particular circumstances of the company.		
	The audit committee should review annually its terms of reference and its own effectiveness and recommend any necessary changes to the board.		
	The board should review the audit committee's effectiveness annually.		
	Where disagreements between the audit committee and the board cannot be resolved, the audit committee should have the right to report the issue to the shareholders as part of the report on its activities in the annual report.		
Financial reporting	The audit committee should review the significant financial reporting issues, judgements, and clarity and completeness of disclosures made in connection with the preparation of the company's financial statements, interim reports, preliminary announcements and	The audit committee must review: • major issues regarding accounting principles and financial statement presentations, including any significant changes in company's selection or application of accounting principles;	The external auditor must report on a timely basis to the audit committee: • all critical accounting policies and practices applied in its financial statements and the auditors assessment of managements disclosures regarding such policies and practices;

Smith Guidance for Audit Committees	NYSE Audit Committee Regulations	SEC Audit Committee Regulations
related formal statements such as the Operating and Financial Review recommended.	• major issues as to adequacy of company's internal controls and any special audit steps adopted in light of material control deficiencies; • analysis prepared by management and/or external auditors setting forth – significant financial reporting issues and judgments; – effects of alternative GAAP methods on the financial statements; • the effect of regulatory and accounting initiatives, as well as off-balance sheet structures, on the financial statements; and • earnings press releases (paying particular attention to any use of 'pro forma' or 'adjusted' non GAAP information), as well as the financial information and earnings guidance provided to analysts and rating agencies. Discuss annual and quarterly financial statements, including the MD&A with management and external auditors.	• GAAP alternatives discussed with management and the alternative preferred by the audit firm; • other material written communications with management such as the management letter and unadjusted audit differences; and • initial selection of and changes in significant accounting policies, or their application, occurring during the current audit period.

	Smith Guidance for Audit Committees	NYSE Audit Committee Regulations	SEC Audit Committee Regulations
		Discuss earnings press releases, financial information and guidance provided to analysts and rating agencies. Discuss risk assessment and risk management policies set by management, and actions taken by management to monitor and control those risks.	
Internal financial control and risk management	The audit committee should review the company's internal financial controls. The audit committee, unless expressly addressed by a separate board risk committee comprised of independent directors or by the board itself, should review the company's internal control and risk management systems. Management is responsible for the identification, assessment, management and monitoring of risk, for developing, operating and monitoring the system of internal control and for providing assurance to the board that it has done so. Except where the board or a risk	The audit committee should discuss the policies that govern the company's risk assessment and risk management, including the company's major financial risks and actions taken by management to monitor and control those risks.	No detailed requirements for audit committees, other than their mandate to assist the board in the oversight of accounting and financial reporting processes, and the effectiveness of financial reporting controls. In certain cases, the audit committee's mandate may well extend to cover oversight of the processes adopted in response to Sarbanes-Oxley section 302 (Disclosure controls and procedures) and section 404 (assessment of internal controls and procedures for financial reporting).

Smith Guidance for Audit Committees	NYSE Audit Committee Regulations	SEC Audit Committee Regulations
committee is expressly responsible for reviewing the effectiveness of the internal control and risk management systems, the audit committee should receive reports from management on the effectiveness of the systems they have established and the results of any testing carried out by internal and external auditors. Except to the extent that this is expressly dealt with by the board or risk committee, the audit committee should review and approve the statements included in the annual report in relation to internal financial control and the management of risk.		
Whistle-blowing: The audit committee should review arrangements by which staff may, in confidence, raise concerns about possible improprieties in matters of financial reporting, financial control or any other matters.	Audit committees must establish procedures for the receipt, retention and treatment of complaints received by the company concerning accounting, internal controls or auditing matters.	Audit committees must establish procedures for the receipt, retention and treatment of complaints received by the company concerning accounting, internal controls or auditing matters.

	Smith Guidance for Audit Committees	NYSE Audit Committee Regulations	SEC Audit Committee Regulations
	The audit committee's objective should be to ensure that arrangements are in place for the proportionate and independent investigation of such matters and for appropriate follow-up action.	The procedures must encompass the confidential, anonymous submission by employees of concerns on questionable accounting and auditing matters.	The procedures must encompass the confidential, anonymous submission by employees of concerns on questionable accounting and auditing matters.
Internal audit	The audit committee should monitor and review the effectiveness of the company's internal audit activities. Where there is no internal audit function, the audit committee should consider annually whether there is a need for an internal audit function and make a recommendation to the board, and the reasons for the absence of such a function should be explained in the relevant section of the annual report. The audit committee should review and approve the internal audit function's remit, having regard to the need for the internal and external audit functions to complement one another.	The audit committee should periodically meet with the internal auditor. Listed companies must maintain an internal audit function to provide management and the audit committee with ongoing assessments of the company's risk management processes and system of internal control. A company may choose to outsource this function to a third-party service provider other than its independent auditor.	

Smith Guidance for Audit Committees	NYSE Audit Committee Regulations	SEC Audit Committee Regulations
The audit committee should approve the appointment or termination of appointment of the head of internal audit. As part of its review work, the audit committee should: • ensure that the internal auditor has direct access to the board chairman and to the audit committee and is accountable to the audit committee; • review and assess the annual internal audit work plan; • receive a report on the results of the internal auditors' work on a periodic basis; • review and monitor management's responsiveness to the internal auditors' findings and recommendations; • meet with the head of internal audit at least once a year without the presence of management; and • monitor and assess the role and effectiveness of the internal audit function in the overall context of the company's risk management system.		

	Smith Guidance for Audit Committees	NYSE Audit Committee Regulations	SEC Audit Committee Regulations
External audit – appointment, terms and remuneration	The audit committee is responsible for overseeing the company's relations with the external auditor.	The audit committee must oversee the auditor's work.	The audit committee must oversee the auditor's work.
	The audit committee should have primary responsibility for making a recommendation to the board on the appointment, reappointment and removal of the external auditors.	The audit committee is responsible for the appointment, compensation, and retention of the auditor.	The audit committee is 'directly responsible to hire, pay and, if necessary, dismiss the independent auditor'.
	If the board does not accept the audit committee's recommendation, it should include in the annual report, and in any papers recommending appointment or reappointment, a statement from the audit committee explaining its recommendation and the reasons why the board has taken a different stance.		
	The audit committee should annually assess the qualification, expertise and resources, effectiveness and independence of the external auditors and the effectiveness of the audit process.	The audit committee should also assess the independent auditor's qualifications, performance and independence. In making its evaluation, the audit committee should consider auditor rotation, the opinions of management, and the company's internal auditors. The audit committee's conclusions should be presented to the full board.	
	The audit committee should approve the terms of engagement and the		

	Smith Guidance for Audit Committees	NYSE Audit Committee Regulations	SEC Audit Committee Regulations
	remuneration to be paid to the external auditor in respect of audit services provided. It should satisfy itself that the level of fee payable in respect of the audit services provided is appropriate and that an effective audit can be conducted for such a fee.		
External audit – independence	The audit committee should assess the procedures in place to ensure the independence and objectivity of the external auditor annually.	The audit committee should obtain and review at least annually a report from the independent auditors that describes the audit firm's quality control procedures, all relationships between the independent auditor and the company, and material issues raised by the firm's most recent internal quality control review or by any governmental or professional inquiry or investigation in the most recent five years relating to the firm's audits.	It is the responsibility of the audit committee to pre-approve all audit and non-audit services provided by the accountant.
	The audit committee should develop and recommend to the board a policy in relation to the provision of non-audit services by the auditor.	The audit committee must have sole authority to approve all significant non-audit engagements with the external auditors.	

	Smith Guidance for Audit Committees	NYSE Audit Committee Regulations	SEC Audit Committee Regulations
	The annual report should explain to shareholders how, if the auditor provides non-audit services, auditor objectivity and independence is safeguarded.		
External audit – annual audit cycle	At the start of each annual audit cycle, the audit committee should ensure that appropriate plans are in place for the audit. The audit committee should review, with the external auditors, the findings of their work. At the end of the annual audit cycle, the audit committee should assess the effectiveness of the audit process.	The audit committee should meet periodically with the independent auditor. Discuss with the independent auditor any problems or difficulties that were encountered during the course of the audit and any significant disagreements with management. The audit committee may review, for example, waived audit adjustments, communications between the audit team and the audit firm's national office, and internal control matters.	The external auditor should report directly to the audit committee. The audit committee should ensure resolution of disagreements between management and the external auditor regarding financial reporting.
Dialogue with shareholders	The terms of reference of the audit committee including its role and the authority delegated to it by the board, should be made available. A separate section in the annual report should describe the work of the committee in discharging those responsibilities.	Audit committees must have a written charter that addresses: • purpose of the audit committee; and • duties and responsibilities of the audit committee.	The audit committee must provide a report disclosing the following: • the audit committee has reviewed and discussed the audited financial statements with management; • discussed certain matters with the independents auditors;

Smith Guidance for Audit Committees	NYSE Audit Committee Regulations	SEC Audit Committee Regulations
This should include: • a summary of the audit committee's role; • the names and qualifications of all members of the audit committee during the period; • the number of audit committee meetings, and who attended them; • a report on how the committee has discharged its duties; and • an explanation of how auditor objectivity and independence is safeguarded. Where disagreements between the audit committee and the board cannot be resolved, the audit committee should have the right to report the issue to the shareholders as part of the report on its activities in the company's annual report. If the board does not accept the audit committee's recommendation regarding the appointment, reappointment and removal of the external auditors, a	The charter must be posted on the company website. The SEC requires disclosure of whether the audit committee has at least one financial expert. If an audit committee does not have a financial expert the reason why must be disclosed.	• whether the audit committee is governed by a charter (if so, this should be appended to the proxy statement every three years); and • whether the members of the audit committee are independent. In addition, the SEC requires disclosure of whether the audit committee has at least one financial expert. If an audit committee does not have a financial expert the reason why must be disclosed.

Smith Guidance for Audit Committees	NYSE Audit Committee Regulations	SEC Audit Committee Regulations
statement from the audit committee explaining its recommendation and reasons why the board has taken a different stance should be included in the annual report.

The annual report should explain to shareholders how the policy in relation to the provision of non-audit services by the auditor provides adequate protection of auditor independence.

The chairman of the audit committee should be present at the AGM to answer questions, through the chairman of the board, on the report on the audit committee's activities and matters within the scope of audit committee's responsibilities. | Each listed company CEO must certify to the NYSE each year that he or she is not aware of any violation by the company of NYSE corporate governance listing standards. This certification must be disclosed in the company's annual report to shareholders. | |

Appendix 16 Financial reporting deadlines

		Public company				Private limited company
	Reference[1]	LSE official list	AIM listed	OFEX	Unlisted	
Announce/ publish annual accounts, directors' report and directors' remuneration report (quoted companies only[2]).		Preliminary announcement (audited or unaudited) within 120 days of the period end. Publish audited results within six months of the period end. *Listing rules: 12.42(e) and 12.48*	Publish and send to shareholders audited results within six months of the period end. *AIM rules, 16 and 17*	Announce audited results within five months of the period end. *OFEX rules: 9.9 and 9.10*	n/a	n/a
Provide copy of the annual accounts, directors' report, directors' remuneration	S238(1) CA 85	Not less than 21 days before the general meeting. Combined Code recommends notice and	Not less than 21 days before the general meeting.	Not less than 21 days before the general meeting.	Not less than 21 days before the general meeting.	Subject to exceptions not less than 21 days before the general meeting[3].

	Reference[1]	Public company				Private limited company
		LSE official list	AIM listed	OFEX	Unlisted	
report and notice of AGM to the members (and others as specified).		papers to be sent to shareholders at least 20 working days before the meeting.				
Hold AGM.	S366(1)&(3) S366A(1) CA 85	Every calendar year not more than 15 months apart.	Every calendar year not more than 15 months apart.	Every calendar year not more than 15 months apart.	Every calendar year not more than 15 months apart.	Every calendar year not more than 15 months apart. Can elect not to have an AGM.
Laying and delivering accounts[4].	S244(1) CA 85	7 months	7 months	7 months	7 months	10 months
Lodge annual return with registrar of companies.	S363 CA 85 Combined Code provision D.2.4	Complete within 28 days of the return date[5].	Complete within 28 days of the return date.	Complete within 28 days of the return date.	Complete within 28 days of the return date.	Complete within 28 days of the return date.

	Reference[1]	Public company			Unlisted	Private limited company
		LSE official list	AIM listed	OFEX		
Announce/publish interim accounts and reports[6].		Publish results within 90 days of the period end17.	Prepare and notify results within three months of the period end	Announce results within three months of the period end18.	n/a	n/a

1 Section references do not apply to Northern Ireland that has separate (but similar) legislation.

2 Quoted companies are those companies whose equity share capital is quoted on the official list of the LSE, the official list in another EEA state, the NYSE or Nasdaq (i.e. not AIM or OFEX companies).

3 Where the company is a small company that is exempt from the requirement to have its accounts audited [S249A, S249E] in respect of a financial year, and has taken advantage of that exemption, it is not required to lay or send to members a copy of the auditor's report. Where the company has by elective resolution dispensed with the laying of accounts and reports before the company in general meetings [S252], copies must be sent out not less than 28 days before the end of the period [S253] allowing for laying and delivering accounts and reports.

4 Where a company carries on business, or has interests, outside of the UK, the directors may claim (by giving notice to the registrar of companies in the prescribed format) a three-month extension to the period allowed for laying and delivering the accounts [S244(3)].

5 The return date is generally the anniversary of incorporation or the date the previous return made up to (where changed in accordance with S363).

6 It is at the discretion of the company whether their external auditors review the interim statements.

7 If the company's external auditors review the interim statements, the auditors' report therein is required to be included in the interim statments.

8 OFEX start-up companies must produce unaudited results on a quality basis during the first three years of the admission.

151

Appendix 17
US Financial expert decision tree

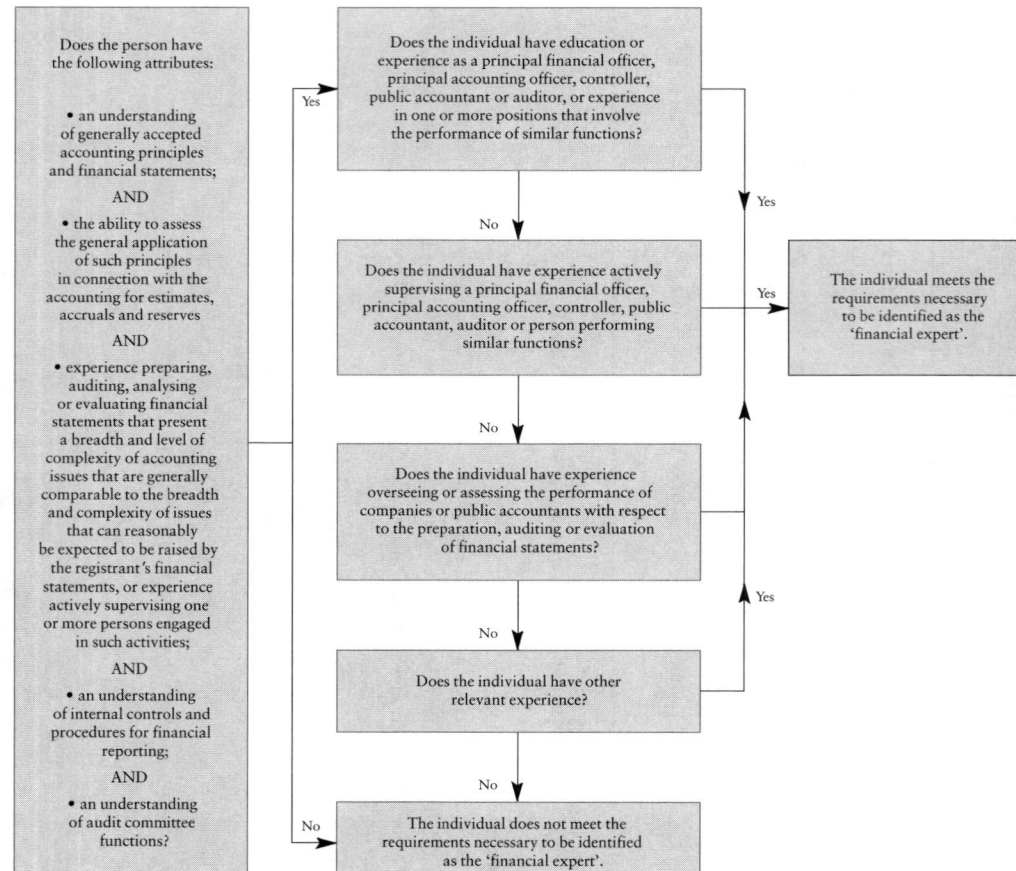

Does the person have the following attributes:

- an understanding of generally accepted accounting principles and financial statements;

AND

- the ability to assess the general application of such principles in connection with the accounting for estimates, accruals and reserves

AND

- experience preparing, auditing, analysing or evaluating financial statements that present a breadth and level of complexity of accounting issues that are generally comparable to the breadth and complexity of issues that can reasonably be expected to be raised by the registrant's financial statements, or experience actively supervising one or more persons engaged in such activities;

AND

- an understanding of internal controls and procedures for financial reporting;

AND

- an understanding of audit committee functions?

Yes

Does the individual have education or experience as a principal financial officer, principal accounting officer, controller, public accountant or auditor, or experience in one or more positions that involve the performance of similar functions?

No

Yes

Does the individual have experience actively supervising a principal financial officer, principal accounting officer, controller, public accountant, auditor or person performing similar functions?

No

Yes

Does the individual have experience overseeing or assessing the performance of companies or public accountants with respect to the preparation, auditing or evaluation of financial statements?

No

Yes

Does the individual have other relevant experience?

No

The individual meets the requirements necessary to be identified as the 'financial expert'.

No

The individual does not meet the requirements necessary to be identified as the 'financial expert'.

Appendix 18
Guidance on audit committees (the Smith Guidance)

Note: The following guidance is closely based on Sir Robert Smith's proposed guidance published in January 2003, modified for consistency with the final revised Code.

Audit Committees – Combined Code Guidance

1   Introduction

1.1   This guidance is designed to assist company boards in making suitable arrangements for their audit committees, and to assist directors serving on audit committees in carrying out their role.

1.2   The paragraphs in bold are taken from the Combined Code (Section C3). Listed companies that do not comply with those provisions should include an explanation as to why they have not complied in the statement required by the Listing Rules.

1.3   Best practice requires that every board should consider in detail what arrangements for its audit committee are best suited for its particular circumstances. Audit committee arrangements need to be proportionate to the task, and will vary according to the size, complexity and risk profile of the company.

1.4   While all directors have a duty to act in the interests of the company the audit committee has a particular role, acting independently of the executive, to ensure that the interests of shareholders are properly protected in relation to financial reporting and internal control.

1.5   Nothing in the guidance should be interpreted as a departure from the principle of the unitary board. All directors remain equally responsible for the company's affairs as a matter of law. The audit committee, like other committees to which particular responsibilities are delegated (such as the remuneration committee), remains a committee of the board. Any disagreement within the board, including disagreement between the audit committee's members and the rest of the board, should be resolved at board level.

1.6   The Code provides that a separate section of the annual report should describe the work of the committee. This deliberately puts the spotlight on the audit committee and gives it an authority that it might otherwise lack. This is not incompatible with the principle of the unitary board.

1.7   The guidance contains recommendations about the conduct of the audit committee's relationship with the board, with the executive management and with internal and external auditors. However, the most important features of this relationship cannot be drafted as guidance or put into a code of practice: a frank, open, working relationship and a high level of mutual respect are essential, particularly between the audit committee chairman and the board chairman, the chief executive and the finance director. The audit committee must be prepared to take a robust stand, and all parties must be prepared to make information freely available to the audit committee, to listen to its views and to talk through the issues openly.

1.8 In particular, the management is under an obligation to ensure the audit committee is kept properly informed, and should take the initiative in supplying information rather than waiting to be asked. The board should make it clear to all directors and staff that they must cooperate with the audit committee and provide it with any information it requires. In addition, executive board members will have regard to their common law duty to provide all directors, including those on the audit committee, with all the information they need to discharge their responsibilities as directors of the company.

1.9 Many of the core functions of audit committees set out in this guidance are expressed in terms of 'oversight', 'assessment' and 'review' of a particular function. It is not the duty of audit committees to carry out functions that properly belong to others, such as the company's management in the preparation of the financial statements or the auditors in the planning or conducting of audits. To do so could undermine the responsibility of management and auditors. Audit committees should, for example, satisfy themselves that there is a proper system and allocation of responsibilities for the day-to-day monitoring of financial controls but they should not seek to do the monitoring themselves.

1.10 However, the high-level oversight function may lead to detailed work. The audit committee must intervene if there are signs that something may be seriously amiss. For example, if the audit committee is uneasy about the explanations of management and auditors about a particular financial reporting policy decision, there may be no alternative but to grapple with the detail and perhaps to seek independent advice.

1.11 Under this guidance, audit committees have wide-ranging, time-consuming and sometimes intensive work to do. Companies need to make the necessary resources available. This includes suitable payment for the members of audit committees themselves. They – and particularly the audit committee chairman – bear a significant responsibility and they need to commit a significant extra amount of time to the job. Companies also need to make provision for induction and training for new audit committee members and continuing training as may be required.

1.12 This guidance applies to all companies to which the Code applies – i.e. UK listed companies. For groups, it will usually be necessary for the audit committee of the parent company to review issues that relate to particular subsidiaries or activities carried on by the group. Consequently, the board of a UK-listed parent company should ensure that there is adequate cooperation within the group (and with internal and external auditors of individual companies within the group) to enable the parent company audit committee to discharge its responsibilities effectively.

2   **Establishment and role of the audit committee; membership, procedures and resources**

Establishment and role

2.1   The board should establish an audit committee of at least three, or in the case of smaller companies two, members.

2.2   The main role and responsibilities of the audit committee should be set out in written terms of reference and should include:
   - to monitor the integrity of the financial statements of the company and any formal announcements relating to the company's financial performance, reviewing significant financial reporting judgements contained in them;
   - to review the company's internal financial controls and, unless expressly addressed by a separate board risk committee composed of independent directors or by the board itself, the company's internal control and risk management systems;
   - to monitor and review the effectiveness of the company's internal audit function;
   - to make recommendations to the board, for it to put to the shareholders for their approval in general meeting, in relation to the appointment of the external auditor and to approve the remuneration and terms of engagement of the external auditor;
   - to review and monitor the external auditor's independence and objectivity and the effectiveness of the audit process, taking into consideration relevant UK professional and regulatory requirements;
   - to develop and implement policy on the engagement of the external auditor to supply non-audit services, taking into account relevant ethical guidance regarding the provision of non-audit services by the external audit firm; and
   - to report to the Board, identifying any matters in respect of which it considers that action or improvement is needed, and making recommendations as to the steps to be taken.

Membership and appointment

2.3   All members of the committee should be independent non-executive directors. The board should satisfy itself that at least one member of the audit committee has recent and relevant financial experience.

2.4   The chairman of the company should not be an audit committee member.

2.5   Appointments to the audit committee should be made by the board on the recommendation of the nomination committee (where there is one), in consultation with the audit committee chairman.

2.6   Appointments should be for a period of up to three years, extendable by no more than two additional three-year periods, so long as members continue to be independent.

Meetings of the audit committee

2.7   It is for the audit committee chairman, in consultation with the company secretary, to decide the frequency and timing of its meetings. There should be as many meetings as the audit committee's role and responsibilities require. It is recommended there should be not fewer than three meetings during the year, held to coincide with key dates within the financial reporting and audit cycle.[1] However, most audit committee chairmen will wish to call more frequent meetings.

2.8 No one other than the audit committee's chairman and members is entitled to be present at a meeting of the audit committee. It is for the audit committee to decide if non-members should attend for a particular meeting or a particular agenda item. It is to be expected that the external audit lead partner will be invited regularly to attend meetings as well as the finance director. Others may be invited to attend.

2.9 Sufficient time should be allowed to enable the audit committee to undertake as full a discussion as may be required. A sufficient interval should be allowed between audit committee meetings and main board meetings to allow any work arising from the audit committee meeting to be carried out and reported to the board as appropriate.

2.10 The audit committee should, at least annually, meet the external and internal auditors, without management, to discuss matters relating to its remit and any issues arising from the audit.

2.11 Formal meetings of the audit committee are the heart of its work. However, they will rarely be sufficient. It is expected that the audit committee chairman, and to a lesser extent the other members, will wish to keep in touch on a continuing basis with the key people involved in the company's governance, including the board chairman, the chief executive, the finance director, the external audit lead partner and the head of internal audit.

Resources

2.12 The audit committee should be provided with sufficient resources to undertake its duties.

2.13 The audit committee should have access to the services of the company secretariat on all audit committee matters including: assisting the chairman in planning the audit committee's work, drawing up meeting agendas, maintenance of minutes, drafting of material about its activities for the annual report, collection and distribution of information and provision of any necessary practical support.

2.14 The company secretary should ensure that the audit committee receives information and papers in a timely manner to enable full and proper consideration to be given to the issues.

2.15 The board should make funds available to the audit committee to enable it to take independent legal, accounting or other advice when the audit committee reasonably believes it necessary to do so.

Remuneration

2.16 In addition to the remuneration paid to all non-executive directors, each company should consider the further remuneration that should be paid to members of the audit

---

1 For example, when the aduit plans (internal and external) are available for review and when interim statements, preliminary announcements and the full annual report are near completion.

committee to recompense them for the additional responsibilities of membership. Consideration should be given to the time members are required to give to audit committee business, the skills they bring to bear and the onerous duties they take on, as well as the value of their work to the company. The level of remuneration paid to the members of the audit committee should take into account the level of fees paid to other members of the board. The chairman's responsibilities and time demands will generally be heavier than the other members of the audit committee and this should be reflected in his or her remuneration.

Skills, experience and training

2.17 It is desirable that the committee member whom the board considers to have recent and relevant financial experience should have a professional qualification from one of the professional accountancy bodies. The need for a degree of financial literacy among the other members will vary according to the nature of the company, but experience of corporate financial matters will normally be required. The availability of appropriate financial expertise will be particularly important where the company's activities involve specialised financial activities.

2.18 The company should provide an induction programme for new audit committee members. This should cover the role of the audit committee, including its terms of reference and expected time commitment by members; and an overview of the company's business, identifying the main business and financial dynamics and risks. It could also include meeting some of the company staff.

2.19 Training should also be provided to members of the audit committee on an ongoing and timely basis and should include an understanding of the principles of and developments in financial reporting and related company law. In appropriate cases, it may also include, for example, understanding financial statements, applicable accounting standards and recommended practice; the regulatory framework for the company's business; the role of internal and external auditing and risk management.

2.20 The induction programme and ongoing training may take various forms, including attendance at formal courses and conferences, internal company talks and seminars, and briefings by external advisers.

3 Relationship with the board

3.1 The role of the audit committee is for the board to decide and to the extent that the audit committee undertakes tasks on behalf of the board, the results should be reported to, and considered by, the board. In doing so it should identify any matters in respect of which it considers that action or improvement is needed, and make recommendations as to the steps to be taken.

3.2 The terms of reference should be tailored to the particular circumstances of the company.

3.3 The audit committee should review annually its terms of reference and its own effectiveness and recommend any necessary changes to the board.

3.4   The board should review the audit committee's effectiveness annually.

3.5   Where there is disagreement between the audit committee and the board, adequate time should be made available for discussion of the issue with a view to resolving the disagreement. Where any such disagreements cannot be resolved, the audit committee should have the right to report the issue to the shareholders as part of the report on its activities in the annual report.

4   Role and responsibilities

Financial reporting

4.1   The audit committee should review the significant financial reporting issues and judgements made in connection with the preparation of the company's financial statements, interim reports, preliminary announcements and related formal statements.

4.2   It is management's, not the audit committee's, responsibility to prepare complete and accurate financial statements and disclosures in accordance with financial reporting standards and applicable rules and regulations. However, the audit committee should consider significant accounting policies, any changes to them and any significant estimates and judgements. The management should inform the audit committee of the methods used to account for significant or unusual transactions where the accounting treatment is open to different approaches. Taking into account the external auditor's view, the audit committee should consider whether the company has adopted appropriate accounting policies and, where necessary, made appropriate estimates and judgements. The audit committee should review the clarity and completeness of disclosures in the financial statements and consider whether the disclosures made are set properly in context.

4.3   Where, following its review, the audit committee is not satisfied with any aspect of the proposed financial reporting by the company, it shall report its views to the board.

4.4   The audit committee should review related information presented with the financial statements, including the operating and financial review, and corporate governance statements relating to the audit and to risk management. Similarly, where board approval is required for other statements containing financial information (for example, summary financial statements, significant financial returns to regulators and release of price sensitive information), whenever practicable (without being inconsistent with any requirement for prompt reporting under the Listing Rules) the audit committee should review such statements first.

Internal controls and risk management systems

4.5   The audit committee should review the company's internal financial controls (that is, the systems established to identify, assess, manage and monitor financial risks); and unless expressly addressed by a separate board risk committee comprised of independent directors or by the board itself, the company's internal control and risk management systems.

4.6　The company's management is responsible for the identification, assessment, management and monitoring of risk, for developing, operating and monitoring the system of internal control and for providing assurance to the board that it has done so. Except where the board or a risk committee is expressly responsible for reviewing the effectiveness of the internal control and risk management systems, the audit committee should receive reports from management on the effectiveness of the systems they have established and the conclusions of any testing carried out by internal and external auditors.

4.7　Except to the extent that this is expressly dealt with by the board or risk committee, the audit committee should review and approve the statements included in the annual report in relation to internal control and the management of risk.

Whistleblowing

4.8　The audit committee should review arrangements by which staff of the company may, in confidence, raise concerns about possible improprieties in matters of financial reporting or other matters. The audit committee's objective should be to ensure that arrangements are in place for the proportionate and independent investigation of such matters and for appropriate follow-up action.

The internal audit process

4.9　The audit committee should monitor and review the effectiveness of the company's internal audit function. Where there is no internal audit function, the audit committee should consider annually whether there is a need for an internal audit function and make a recommendation to the board, and the reasons for the absence of such a function should be explained in the relevant section of the annual report.

4.10　The audit committee should review and approve the internal audit function's remit, having regard to the complementary roles of the internal and external audit functions. The audit committee should ensure that the function has the necessary resources and access to information to enable it to fulfil its mandate, and is equipped to perform in accordance with appropriate professional standards for internal auditors.[2]

4.11　The audit committee should approve the appointment or termination of appointment of the head of internal audit.

4.12　In its review of the work of the internal audit function, the audit committee should, *inter alia*:
- ensure that the internal auditor has direct access to the board chairman and to the audit committee and is accountable to the audit committee;
- review and assess the annual internal audit work plan;
- receive a report on the results of the internal auditors' work on a periodic basis;
- review and monitor management's responsiveness to the internal auditor's findings and recommendations;
- meet with the head of internal audit at least once a year without the presence of management; and

2 Further guidance can by found in the Institute of Internal Auditors' Code of Ethics and the International Standards for the Professional Practice of Internal Auditing Standards.

- monitor and assess the role and effectiveness of the internal audit function in the overall context of the company's risk management system.

The external audit process

4.13 The audit committee is the body responsible for overseeing the company's relations with the external auditor.

Appointment

4.14 The audit committee should have primary responsibility for making a recommendation on the appointment, reappointment and removal of the external auditors. If the board does not accept the audit committee's recommendation, it should include in the annual report, and in any papers recommending appointment or reappointment, a statement from the audit committee explaining its recommendation and should set out reasons why the board has taken a different position.

4.15 The audit committee's recommendation to the board should be based on the assessments referred to below. If the audit committee recommends considering the selection of possible new appointees as external auditors, it should oversee the selection process.

4.16 The audit committee should assess annually the qualification, expertise and resources, and independence (see below) of the external auditors and the effectiveness of the audit process. The assessment should cover all aspects of the audit service provided by the audit firm, and include obtaining a report on the audit firm's own internal quality control procedures.

4.17 If the external auditor resigns, the audit committee should investigate the issues giving rise to such resignation and consider whether any action is required.

Terms and remuneration

4.18 The audit committee should approve the terms of engagement and the remuneration to be paid to the external auditor in respect of audit services provided.

4.19 The audit committee should review and agree the engagement letter issued by the external auditor at the start of each audit, ensuring that it has been updated to reflect changes in circumstances arising since the previous year. The scope of the external audit should be reviewed by the audit committee with the auditor. If the audit committee is not satisfied as to its adequacy it should arrange for additional work to be undertaken.

4.20 The audit committee should satisfy itself that the level of fee payable in respect of the audit services provided is appropriate and that an effective audit can be conducted for such a fee.

Independence, including the provision of non-audit services

4.21 The audit committee should have procedures to ensure the independence and objectivity of the external auditor annually, taking into consideration relevant UK professional and regulatory requirements. This assessment should involve a consideration of all relationships between the company and the audit firm (including the provision of non-audit services). The audit committee should consider whether, taken as a whole and having regard to the views, as appropriate, of the external auditor, management and internal audit, those relationships appear to impair the auditor's judgement or independence.

4.22   The audit committee should seek reassurance that the auditors and their staff have no family, financial, employment, investment or business relationship with the company (other than in the normal course of business). The audit committee should seek from the audit firm, on an annual basis, information about policies and processes for maintaining independence and monitoring compliance with relevant requirements, including current requirements regarding the rotation of audit partners and staff.

4.23   The audit committee should agree with the board the company's policy for the employment of former employees of the external auditor, paying particular attention to the policy regarding former employees of the audit firm who were part of the audit team and moved directly to the company. This should be drafted taking into account the relevant ethical guidelines governing the accounting profession. The audit committee should monitor application of the policy, including the number of former employees of the external auditor currently employed in senior positions in the company, and consider whether in the light of this there has been any impairment, or appearance of impairment, of the auditor's judgement or independence in respect of the audit.

4.24   The audit committee should monitor the external audit firm's compliance with applicable United Kingdom ethical guidance relating to the rotation of audit partners, the level of fees that the company pays in proportion to the overall fee income of the firm, office and partner, and other related regulatory requirements.

4.25   The audit committee should develop and recommend to the board the company's policy in relation to the provision of non-audit services by the auditor. The audit committee's objective should be to ensure that the provision of such services does not impair the external auditor's independence or objectivity. In this context, the audit committee should consider:
   * whether the skills and experience of the audit firm make it a suitable supplier of the non audit service;
   * whether there are safeguards in place to ensure that there is no threat to objectivity and independence in the conduct of the audit resulting from the provision of such services by the external auditor;
   * the nature of the non-audit services, the related fee levels and the fee levels individually and in aggregate relative to the audit fee; and
   * the criteria which govern the compensation of the individuals performing the audit.

4.26   The audit committee should set and apply a formal policy specifying the types of non-audit work:
   * from which the external auditors are excluded;
   * for which the external auditors can be engaged without referral to the audit committee; and
   * for which a case-by-case decision is necessary.

In addition, the policy may set fee limits generally or for particular classes of work.

4.27   In the third category, if it is not practicable to give approval to individual items in advance, it may be appropriate to give a general pre-approval for certain classes for work, subject to a fee limit determined by the audit committee and ratified by the board. The subsequent provision of any service by the auditor should be ratified at the next meeting of the audit committee.

4.28   In determining the policy, the audit committee should take into account relevant ethical guidance regarding the provision of non-audit services by the external audit firm, and in principle should not agree to the auditor providing a service if, having regard to the ethical guidance, the result is that:
- the external auditor audits its own firm's work;
- the external auditor makes management decisions for the company;
- a mutuality of interest is created; or
- the external auditor is put in the role of advocate for the company.

The audit committee should satisfy itself that any safeguards required by ethical guidance are implemented.

4.29   The annual report should explain to shareholders how, if the auditor provides non-audit services, auditor objectivity and independence is safeguarded.

Annual audit cycle

4.30   At the start of each annual audit cycle, the audit committee should ensure that appropriate plans are in place for the audit.

4.31   The audit committee should consider whether the auditor's overall work plan, including planned levels of materiality, and proposed resources to execute the audit plan appears consistent with the scope of the audit engagement, having regard also to the seniority, expertise and experience of the audit team.

4.32   The audit committee should review, with the external auditors, the findings of its work. In the course of its review, the audit committee should:
- discuss with the external auditor major issues that arose during the course of the audit and have subsequently been resolved and those issues that have been left unresolved;
- review key accounting and audit judgements; and
- review levels of errors identified during the audit, obtaining explanations from management and, where necessary the external auditors, as to why certain errors might remain unadjusted.

4.33   The audit committee should also review the audit representation letters before signature by management and give particular consideration to matters where representation has been requested that relate to non-standard issues[3]. The audit committee should consider whether the information provided is complete and appropriate based on its own knowledge.

---

3 Further guidance can by found in the Auditing Practices Board's Statement of Auditing Standard 440 'Management Representations'.

4.34 As part of the ongoing monitoring process, the audit committee should review the management letter (or equivalent). The audit committee should review and monitor management's responsiveness to the external auditor's findings and recommendations.

4.35 At the end of the annual audit cycle, the audit committee should assess the effectiveness of the audit process. In the course of doing so, the audit committee should:

- review whether the auditor has met the agreed audit plan, and understand the reasons for any changes, including changes in perceived audit risks and the work undertaken by the external auditors to address those risks;
- consider the robustness and perceptiveness of the auditors in their handling of the key accounting and audit judgements identified and in responding to questions from the audit committees, and in their commentary where appropriate on the systems of internal control;
- obtain feedback about the conduct of the audit from key people involved, e.g. the finance director and the head of internal audit; and
- review and monitor the content of the external auditor's management letter, in order to assess whether it is based on a good understanding of the company's business and establish whether recommendations have been acted upon and, if not, the reasons why they have not been acted upon.

5   Communication with shareholders

5.1 The terms of reference of the audit committee, including its role and the authority delegated to it by the board, should be made available. A separate section in the annual report should describe the work of the committee in discharging those responsibilities.

5.2 The audit committee section should include, *inter alia*:

- a summary of the role of the audit committee;
- the names and qualifications of all members of the audit committee during the period;
- the number of audit committee meetings;
- a report on the way the audit committee has discharged its responsibilities; and
- the explanation provided for in paragraph 4.29 above.

5.3 The chairman of the audit committee should be present at the AGM to answer questions, through the chairman of the board, on the report on the audit committee's activities and matters within the scope of the audit committee's responsibilities.

Appendix 19
Guidance on internal control (the Turnbull Guidance)

Note: Principle D.2, provision D.2.1 and provision D.2.2 of the old (1998) Code appear in the new (2003) Code as principle C.2, provision C.2.1 and (in an amended form) provision C.3.5. The Code references in the guidance on internal control should be read accordingly.

Introudction

Internal control requirements of the Combined Code

1   When the Combined Code of the Committee on Corporate Governance (the Code) was published, the Institute of Chartered Accountants in England & Wales agreed with the London Stock Exchange that it would provide guidance to assist listed companies to implement the requirements in the Code relating to internal control.

2   Principle D.2 of the Code states that 'The board should maintain a sound system of internal control to safeguard shareholders' investment and the company's assets'.

3   Provision D.2.1 states that 'The directors should, at least annually, conduct a review of the effectiveness of the group's system of internal control and should report to shareholders that they have done so. The review should cover all controls, including financial, operational and compliance controls and risk management'.

4   Provision D.2.2 states that 'Companies which do not have an internal audit function should from time to time review the need for one'.

5   Paragraph 12.43A of the London Stock Exchange Listing Rules states that 'in the case of a company incorporated in the United Kingdom, the following additional items must be included in its annual report and accounts:
    (a)   a narrative statement of how it has applied the principles set out in Section 1 of the Combined Code, providing explanation which enables its shareholders to evaluate how the principles have been applied;
    (b)   a statement as to whether or not it has complied throughout the accounting period with the Code provisions set out in Section 1 of the Combined Code. A company that has not complied with the Code provisions, or complied with only some of the Code provisions or (in the case of provisions whose requirements are of a continuing nature) complied for only part of an accounting period, must specify the Code provisions with which it has not complied, and (where relevant) for what part of the period such non-compliance continued, and give reasons for any non-compliance.

6   The Preamble to the Code, which is appended to the Listing Rules, makes it clear that there is no prescribed form or content for the statement setting out how the various principles in the Code have been applied. The intention is that companies should have a free

hand to explain their governance policies in the light of the principles, including any special circumstances which have led to them adopting a particular approach.

7   The guidance in this document should be followed by boards of listed companies in:
- assessing how the company has applied Code principle D.2;
- implementing the requirements of Code provisions D.2.1 and D.2.2; and
- reporting on these matters to shareholders in the annual report and accounts.

Objectives of the guidance

8   This guidance is intended to:
- reflect sound business practice whereby internal control is embedded in the business processes by which a company pursues its objectives;
- remain relevant over time in the continually evolving business environment; and
- enable each company to apply it in a manner which takes account of its particular circumstances.

The guidance requires directors to exercise judgement in reviewing how the company has implemented the requirements of the Code relating to internal control and reporting to shareholders thereon.

9   The guidance is based on the adoption by a company's board of a risk-based approach to establishing a sound system of internal control and reviewing its effectiveness. This should be incorporated by the company within its normal management and governance processes. It should not be treated as a separate exercise undertaken to meet regulatory requirements.

The importance of internal control and risk management

10   A company's system of internal control has a key role in the management of risks that are significant to the fulfilment of its business objectives. A sound system of internal control contributes to safeguarding the shareholders' investment and the company's assets.

11   Internal control (as referred to in paragraph 20) facilitates the effectiveness and efficiency of operations, helps ensure the reliability of internal and external reporting and assists compliance with laws and regulations.

12   Effective financial controls, including the maintenance of proper accounting records, are an important element of internal control. They help ensure that the company is not unnecessarily exposed to avoidable financial risks and that financial information used within the business and for publication is reliable. They also contribute to the safeguarding of assets, including the prevention and detection of fraud.

13   A company's objectives, its internal organisation and the environment in which it operates are continually evolving and, as a result, the risks it faces are continually changing. A sound system of internal control therefore depends on a thorough and regular evaluation of the nature and extent of the risks to which the company is exposed. Since profits are, in part, the reward for successful risk-taking in business, the purpose of internal control is to help manage and control risk appropriately rather than to eliminate it.

Groups of companies

14 Throughout this guidance, where reference is made to 'company' it should be taken, where applicable, as referring to the group of which the reporting company is the parent company. For groups of companies, the review of effectiveness of internal control and the report to the shareholders should be from the perspective of the group as a whole.

The appendix

15 The appendix to this document contains questions which boards may wish to consider in applying this guidance.

Maintaining a sound system of internal control

Responsibilities

16 The board of directors is responsible for the company's system of internal control. It should set appropriate policies on internal control and seek regular assurance that will enable it to satisfy itself that the system is functioning effectively. The board must further ensure that the system of internal control is effective in managing risks in the manner which it has approved.

17 In determining its policies with regard to internal control, and thereby assessing what constitutes a sound system of internal control in the particular circumstances of the company, the board's deliberations should include consideration of the following factors:
- the nature and extent of the risks facing the company;
- the extent and categories of risk which it regards as acceptable for the company to bear;
- the likelihood of the risks concerned materialising;
- the company's ability to reduce the incidence and impact on the business of risks that do materialise; and
- the costs of operating particular controls relative to the benefit thereby obtained in managing the related risks.

18 It is the role of management to implement board policies on risk and control. In fulfilling its responsibilities, management should identify and evaluate the risks faced by the company for consideration by the board and design, operate and monitor a suitable system of internal control which implements the policies adopted by the board.

19 All employees have some responsibility for internal control as part of their accountability for achieving objectives. They, collectively, should have the necessary knowledge, skills, information and authority to establish, operate and monitor the system of internal control. This will require an understanding of the company, its objectives, the industries and markets in which it operates, and the risks it faces.

Elements of a sound system of internal control

20 An internal control system encompasses the policies, processes, tasks, behaviours and other aspects of a company that, taken together:
- facilitate its effective and efficient operation by enabling it to respond appropriately to significant business, operational, financial, compliance and other risks to achieving the company's objectives. This includes the safeguarding of assets from inappropriate use or from loss and fraud, and ensuring that liabilities are identified and managed;
- help ensure the quality of internal and external reporting. This requires the maintenance of proper records and processes that generate a flow of timely, relevant and reliable information from within and outside the organisation; and
- help ensure compliance with applicable laws and regulations, and also with internal policies with respect to the conduct of business.

21 A company's system of internal control will reflect its control environment which encompasses its organisational structure. The system will include:
- control activities;
- information and communications processes; and
- processes for monitoring the continuing effectiveness of the system of internal control.

22 The system of internal control should:
- be embedded in the operations of the company and form part of its culture;
- be capable of responding quickly to evolving risks to the business arising from factors within the company and to changes in the business environment; and
- include procedures for reporting immediately to appropriate levels of management any significant control failings or weaknesses that are identified together with details of corrective action being undertaken.

23 A sound system of internal control reduces, but cannot eliminate, the possibility of poor judgement in decision-making; human error; control processes being deliberately circumvented by employees and others; management overriding controls; and the occurrence of unforeseeable circumstances.

24 A sound system of internal control therefore provides reasonable, but not absolute, assurance that a company will not be hindered in achieving its business objectives, or in the orderly and legitimate conduct of its business, by circumstances which may reasonably be foreseen. A system of internal control cannot, however, provide protection with certainty against a company failing to meet its business objectives or all material errors, losses, fraud, or breaches of laws or regulations.

Reviewing the effectiveness of internal control

Responsibilities

25 Reviewing the effectiveness of internal control is an essential part of the board's responsibilities. The board will need to form its own view on effectiveness after due and careful enquiry based on the information and assurances provided to it. Management is accountable to the board for monitoring the system of internal control and for providing assurance to the board that it has done so.

26 The role of board committees in the review process, including that of the audit committee, is for the board to decide and will depend upon factors such as the size and composition of the board; the scale, diversity and complexity of the company's operations; and the nature of the significant risks that the company faces. To the extent that designated board committees carry out, on behalf of the board, tasks that are attributed in this guidance document to the board, the results of the relevant committees' work should be reported to, and considered by, the board. The board takes responsibility for the disclosures on internal control in the annual report and accounts.

The process for reviewing effectiveness

27 Effective monitoring on a continuous basis is an essential component of a sound system of internal control. The board cannot, however, rely solely on the embedded monitoring processes within the company to discharge its responsibilities. It should regularly receive and review reports on internal control. In addition, the board should undertake an annual assessment for the purposes of making its public statement on internal control to ensure that it has considered all significant aspects of internal control for the company for the year under review and up to the date of approval of the annual report and accounts.

28 The reference to 'all controls' in Code Provision D.2.1 should not be taken to mean that the effectiveness of every internal control (including controls designed to manage immaterial risks) should be subject to review by the board. Rather it means that, for the purposes of this guidance, internal controls considered by the board should include all types of controls including those of an operational and compliance nature, as well as internal financial controls.

29 The board should define the process to be adopted for its review of the effectiveness of internal control. This should encompass both the scope and frequency of the reports it receives and reviews during the year, and also the process for its annual assessment, such that it will be provided with sound, appropriately documented, support for its statement on internal control in the company's annual report and accounts.

30 The reports from management to the board should, in relation to the areas covered by them, provide a balanced assessment of the significant risks and the effectiveness of the system of internal control in managing those risks. Any significant control failings or weaknesses identified should be discussed in the reports, including the impact that they have had, could have had, or may have, on the company and the actions being taken to

rectify them. It is essential that there be openness of communication by management with the board on matters relating to risk and control.

31 When reviewing reports during the year, the board should:
- consider what are the significant risks and assess how they have been identified, evaluated and managed;
- assess the effectiveness of the related system of internal control in managing the significant risks, having regard, in particular, to any significant failings or weaknesses in internal control that have been reported;
- consider whether necessary actions are being taken promptly to remedy any significant failings or weaknesses; and
- consider whether the findings indicate a need for more extensive monitoring of the system of internal control.

32 Additionally, the board should undertake an annual assessment for the purpose of making its public statement on internal control. The assessment should consider issues dealt with in reports reviewed by it during the year together with any additional information necessary to ensure that the board has taken account of all significant aspects of internal control for the company for the year under review and up to the date of approval of the annual report and accounts.

33 The board's annual assessment should, in particular, consider:
- the changes since the last annual assessment in the nature and extent of significant risks, and the company's ability to respond to changes in its business and the external environment;
- the scope and quality of management's ongoing monitoring of risks and of the system of internal control, and, where applicable, the work of its internal audit function and other providers of assurance;
- the extent and frequency of the communication of the results of the monitoring to the board (or board committee(s)) which enables it to build up a cumulative assessment of the state of control in the company and the effectiveness with which risk is being managed;
- the incidence of significant control failings or weaknesses that have been identified at any time during the period and the extent to which they have resulted in unforeseen outcomes or contingencies that have had, could have had, or may in the future have, a material impact on the company's financial performance or condition; and
- the effectiveness of the company's public reporting processes.

34 Should the board become aware at any time of a significant failing or weakness in internal control, it should determine how the failing or weakness arose and reassess the effectiveness of management's ongoing processes for designing, operating and monitoring the system of internal control.

The board's statement on internal control

35 In its narrative statement of how the company has applied Code principle D.2, the board should, as a minimum, disclose that there is an ongoing process for identifying, evaluat-

ing and managing the significant risks faced by the company, that it has been in place for the year under review and up to the date of approval of the annual report and accounts, that it is regularly reviewed by the board and accords with the guidance in this document.

36   The board may wish to provide additional information in the annual report and accounts to assist understanding of the company's risk management processes and system of internal control.

37   The disclosures relating to the application of principle D.2 should include an acknowledgement by the board that it is responsible for the company's system of internal control and for reviewing its effectiveness. It should also explain that such a system is designed to manage rather than eliminate the risk of failure to achieve business objectives, and can only provide reasonable and not absolute assurance against material misstatement or loss.

38   In relation to Code provision D.2.1, the board should summarise the process it (where applicable, through its committees) has applied in reviewing the effectiveness of the system of internal control. It should also disclose the process it has applied to deal with material internal control aspects of any significant problems disclosed in the annual report and accounts.

39   Where a board cannot make one or more of the disclosures in paragraphs 35 and 38, it should state this fact and provide an explanation. The Listing Rules require the board to disclose if it has failed to conduct a review of the effectiveness of the company's system of internal control.

40   The board should ensure that its disclosures provide meaningful, high-level information and do not give a misleading impression.

41   Where material joint ventures and associates have not been dealt with as part of the group for the purposes of applying this guidance, this should be disclosed.

Internal audit

42   Provision D.2.2 of the Code states that companies which do not have an internal audit function should from time to time review the need for one.

43   The need for an internal audit function will vary depending on company-specific factors including the scale, diversity and complexity of the company's activities and the number of employees, as well as cost/benefit considerations. Senior management and the board may desire objective assurance and advice on risk and control. An adequately resourced internal audit function (or its equivalent where, for example, a third party is contracted to perform some or all of the work concerned) may provide such assurance and advice. There may be other functions within the company that also provide assurance and advice covering specialist areas such as health and safety, regulatory and legal compliance and environmental issues.

44   In the absence of an internal audit function, management needs to apply other monitoring processes in order to assure itself and the board that the system of internal control is

functioning as intended. In these circumstances, the board will need to assess whether such processes provide sufficient and objective assurance.

45 When undertaking its assessment of the need for an internal audit function, the board should also consider whether there are any trends or current factors relevant to the company's activities, markets or other aspects of its external environment, that have increased, or are expected to increase, the risks faced by the company. Such an increase in risk may also arise from internal factors such as organisational restructuring or from changes in reporting processes or underlying information systems. Other matters to be taken into account may include adverse trends evident from the monitoring of internal control systems or an increased incidence of unexpected occurrences.

46 The board of a company that does not have an internal audit function should assess the need for such a function annually having regard to the factors referred to in paragraphs 43 and 45 above. Where there is an internal audit function, the board should annually review its scope of work, authority and resources, again having regard to those factors.

47 If the company does not have an internal audit function and the board has not reviewed the need for one, the Listing Rules require the board to disclose these facts.

Appendix

Assessing the effectiveness of the company's risk and control processes

Some questions which the board may wish to consider and discuss with management when regularly reviewing reports on internal control and carrying out its annual assessment are set out below. The questions are not intended to be exhaustive and will need to be tailored to the particular circumstances of the company.

This appendix should be read in conjunction with the guidance set out in this document.

1   Risk assessment
  • Does the company have clear objectives and have they been communicated so as to provide effective direction to employees on risk assessment and control issues? For example, do objectives and related plans include measurable performance targets and indicators?
  • Are the significant internal and external operational, financial, compliance and other risks identified and assessed on an ongoing basis? (Significant risks may, for example, include those related to market, credit, liquidity, technological, legal, health, safety and environmental, reputation, and business probity issues.)
  • Is there a clear understanding by management and others within the company of what risks are acceptable to the board?

2   Control environment and control activities
  • Does the board have clear strategies for dealing with the significant risks that have been identified? Is there a policy on how to manage these risks?
  • Do the company's culture, code of conduct, human resource policies and performance reward systems support the business objectives and risk management and internal control system?

- Does senior management demonstrate, through its actions as well as its policies, the necessary commitment to competence, integrity and fostering a climate of trust within the company?
- Are authority, responsibility and accountability defined clearly such that decisions are made and actions taken by the appropriate people? Are the decisions and actions of different parts of the company appropriately co-ordinated?
- Does the company communicate to its employees what is expected of them and the scope of their freedom to act? This may apply to areas such as customer relations; service levels for both internal and outsourced activities; health, safety and environmental protection; security of tangible and intangible assets; business continuity issues; expenditure matters; accounting; and financial and other reporting.
- Do people in the company (and in its providers of outsourced services) have the knowledge, skills and tools to support the achievement of the company's objectives and to manage effectively risks to their achievement?
- How are processes/controls adjusted to reflect new or changing risks, or operational deficiencies?

3   Information and communication

- Do management and the board receive timely, relevant and reliable reports on progress against business objectives and the related risks that provide them with the information, from inside and outside the company, needed for decision-making and management review purposes? This could include performance reports and indicators of change, together with qualitative information such as on customer satisfaction, employee attitudes etc.
- Are information needs and related information systems reassessed as objectives and related risks change or as reporting deficiencies are identified?
- Are periodic reporting procedures, including half-yearly and annual reporting, effective in communicating a balanced and understandable account of the company's position and prospects?
- Are there established channels of communication for individuals to report suspected breaches of laws or regulations or other improprieties?

4   Monitoring

- Are there ongoing processes embedded within the company's overall business operations, and addressed by senior management, which monitor the effective application of the policies, processes and activities related to internal control and risk management? (Such processes may include control self-assessment, confirmation by personnel of compliance with policies and codes of conduct, internal audit reviews or other management reviews.)
- Do these processes monitor the company's ability to re-evaluate risks and adjust controls effectively in response to changes in its objectives, its business and its external environment?
- Are there effective follow-up procedures to ensure that appropriate change or action occurs in response to changes in risk and control assessments?

- Is there appropriate communication to the board (or board committees) on the effectiveness of the ongoing monitoring processes on risk and control matters? This should include reporting any significant failings or weaknesses on a timely basis.
- Are there specific arrangements for management monitoring and reporting to the board on risk and control matters of particular importance? These could include, for example, actual or suspected fraud and other illegal or irregular acts, or matters that could adversely affect the company's reputation or financial position.

Appendix 20
The Combined Code on Corporate Governance July 2003

Preamble

1   This Code supersedes and replaces the Combined Code issued by the Hampel Committee on Corporate Governance in June 1998. It derives from a review of the role and effectiveness of non-executive directors by Derek Higgs[1] and a review of audit committees[2] by a group led by Sir Robert Smith.

2   The Financial Services Authority has said that it will replace the 1998 Code that is annexed to the Listing Rules with the revised Code and will seek to make consequential Rule changes. There will be consultation on the necessary Rule changes but not further consultation on the Code provisions themselves.

3   It is intended that the new Code will apply for reporting years beginning on or after 1 November 2003.

4   The Code contains main and supporting principles and provisions. The existing Listing Rules require listed companies to make a disclosure statement in two parts in relation to the Code. In the first part of the statement, the company has to report on how it applies the principles in the Code. In future this will need to cover both main and supporting principles. The form and content of this part of the statement are not prescribed, the intention being that companies should have a free hand to explain their governance policies in the light of the principles, including any special circumstances applying to them which have led to a particular approach. In the second part of the statement the company has either to confirm that it complies with the Code's provisions or – where it does not – to provide an explanation. This 'comply or explain' approach has been in operation for over ten years and the flexibility it offers has been widely welcomed both by company boards and by investors. It is for shareholders and others to evaluate the company's statement.

5   While it is expected that listed companies will comply with the Code's provisions most of the time, it is recognised that departure from the provisions of the Code may be justified in particular circumstances. Every company must review each provision carefully and give a considered explanation if it departs from the Code Provisions.

6   Smaller listed companies, in particular those new to listing, may judge that some of the provisions are disproportionate or less relevant in their case. Some of the provisions do not apply to companies below FTSE 350. Such companies may nonetheless consider that it would be appropriate to adopt the approach in the Code and they are encouraged to consider this. Investment companies typically have a different board structure, which may affect the relevance of particular provisions.

7   Whilst recognising that directors are appointed by shareholders who are the owners of companies, it is important that those concerned with the evaluation of governance should do so with common sense in order to promote partnership and trust, based on mutual understanding. They should pay due regard to companies' individual circumstances and bear in mind in particular the size and complexity of the company and the nature of the risks and challenges it faces. Whilst shareholders have every right to challenge companies' explanations if they are unconvincing, they should not be evaluated in a mechanistic way and departures from the Code should not be automatically treated as breaches. Institutional shareholders and their agents should be careful to respond to the statements from companies in a manner that supports the 'comply or explain' principle. As the principles in Section 2 make clear, institutional shareholders should carefully consider explanations given for departure from the Code and make reasoned judgements in each case. They should put their views to the company and be prepared to enter a dialogue if they do not accept the company's position. Institutional shareholders should be prepared to put such views in writing where appropriate.

8   Nothing in this Code should be taken to override the general requirements of law to treat shareholders equally in access to information.

9   This publication includes guidance on how to comply with particular parts of the Code: first, 'Internal Control: Guidance for Directors on the Combined Code'[3], produced by the Turnbull Committee, which relates to Code Provisions on internal control (C.2 and part of C.3 in the Code); and, second, 'Audit Committees: Combined Code Guidance', produced by the Smith Group, which relates to the provisions on audit committees and auditors (C.3 of the Code). In both cases, the guidance suggests ways of applying the relevant Code principles and of complying with the relevant Code Provisions.

10   In addition, this volume also includes suggestions for good practice from the Higgs Report.

11   The revised Code does not include material in the previous Code on the disclosure of directors' remuneration. This is because The Directors' Remuneration Report Regulations 2002[4] are now in force and supersede the earlier Code Provisions. These require the directors of a company to prepare a remuneration report. It is important that this report is clear, transparent and understandable to shareholders.

Code of Best Practice

SECTION 1 COMPANIES

A. DIRECTORS

A.1 The Board

Main Principle

Every company should be headed by an effective board, which is collectively responsible for the success of the company.

Supporting Principles

The board's role is to provide entrepreneurial leadership of the company within a framework of prudent and effective controls which enables risk to be assessed and managed. The board should set the company's strategic aims, ensure that the necessary financial and human resources are in place for the company to meet its objectives and review management performance. The board should set the company's values and standards and ensure that its obligations to its shareholders and others are understood and met.

All directors must take decisions objectively in the interests of the company.

As part of their role as members of a unitary board, non-executive directors should constructively challenge and help develop proposals on strategy. Non-executive directors should scrutinise the performance of management in meeting agreed goals and objectives and monitor the reporting of performance. They should satisfy themselves on the integrity of financial information and that financial controls and systems of risk management are robust and defensible. They are responsible for determining appropriate levels of remuneration of executive directors and have a prime role in appointing, and where necessary removing, executive directors, and in succession planning.

Code Provisions

A.1.1   The board should meet sufficiently regularly to discharge its duties effectively. There should be a formal schedule of matters specifically reserved for its decision. The annual report should include a statement of how the board operates, including a high level statement of which types of decisions are to be taken by the board and which are to be delegated to management.

A.1.2   The annual report should identify the chairman, the deputy chairman (where there is one), the chief executive, the senior independent director and the chairmen and members of the nomination, audit and remuneration committees. It should also set out the number of meetings of the board and those committees and individual attendance by directors.

A.1.3   The chairman should hold meetings with the non-executive directors without the executives present. Led by the senior independent director, the non-executive directors should meet without the chairman present at least annually to appraise the chairman's performance (as described in A.6.1) and on such other occasions as are deemed appropriate.

A.1.4   Where directors have concerns which cannot be resolved about the running of the company or a proposed action, they should ensure that their concerns are recorded in the board minutes. On resignation, a non-executive director should provide a written statement to the chairman, for circulation to the board, if they have any such concerns.

A.1.5   The company should arrange appropriate insurance cover in respect of legal action against its directors.

A.2 Chairman and chief executive

Main Principle

There should be a clear division of responsibilities at the head of the company between the running of the board and the executive responsibility for the running of the company's business. No one individual should have unfettered powers of decision.

Supporting Principle

The chairman is responsible for leadership of the board, ensuring its effectiveness on all aspects of its role and setting its agenda. The chairman is also responsible for ensuring that the directors receive accurate, timely and clear information. The chairman should ensure effective communication with shareholders. The chairman should also facilitate the effective contribution of non-executive directors in particular and ensure constructive relations between executive and non-executive directors.

Code Provisions

A.2.1   The roles of chairman and chief executive should not be exercised by the same individual. The division of responsibilities between the chairman and chief executive should be clearly established, set out in writing and agreed by the board.

A.2.2   [5] The chairman should on appointment meet the independence criteria set out in A.3.1 below. A chief executive should not go on to be chairman of the same company. If exceptionally a board decides that a chief executive should become chairman, the board should consult major shareholders in advance and should set out its reasons to shareholders at the time of the appointment and in the next annual report.

A.3 Board balance and independence

Main Principle

The board should include a balance of executive and non-executive directors (and in particular independent non-executive directors) such that no individual or small group of individuals can dominate the board's decision taking.

Supporting Principles

The board should not be so large as to be unwieldy. The board should be of sufficient size that the balance of skills and experience is appropriate for the requirements of the business and that changes to the board's composition can be managed without undue disruption. To ensure that power and information are not concentrated in one or two individuals, there should be a strong presence on the board of both executive and non-executive directors. The value of ensuring that committee membership is refreshed and that undue reliance is not placed on particular individuals should be taken into account in deciding chairmanship and membership of committees. No one other than the committee chairman and members is entitled to be present at a meeting of the nomination, audit or remuneration committee, but others may attend at the invitation of the committee.

Code Provisions

A.3.1   The board should identify in the annual report each non-executive director it considers to be independent.[6] The board should determine whether the director is independent in character and judgement and whether there are relationships or circumstances which are likely to affect, or could appear to affect, the director's judgement. The board should state its reasons if it determines that a director is independent notwithstanding the existence of relationships or circumstances which may appear relevant to its determination, including if the director:
- has been an employee of the company or group within the last five years;
- has, or has had within the last three years, a material business relationship with the company either directly, or as a partner, shareholder, director or senior employee of a body that has such a relationship with the company;
- has received or receives additional remuneration from the company apart from a director's fee, participates in the company's share option or a performance-related pay scheme, or is a member of the company's pension scheme;
- has close family ties with any of the company's advisers, directors or senior employees;
- holds cross-directorships or has significant links with other directors through involvement in other companies or bodies;
- represents a significant shareholder; or
- has served on the board for more than nine years from the date of their first election.

A.3.2   Except for smaller companies[7], at least half the board, excluding the chairman, should comprise non-executive directors determined by the board to be independent. A smaller company should have at least two independent non-executive directors.

A.3.3   The board should appoint one of the independent non-executive directors to be the senior independent director. The senior independent director should be available to shareholders if they have concerns which contact through the normal channels of chairman, chief executive or finance director has failed to resolve or for which such contact is inappropriate.

A.4   Appointments to the Board

Main Principle

There should be a formal, rigorous and transparent procedure for the appointment of new directors to the board.

Supporting Principles

Appointments to the board should be made on merit and against objective criteria. Care should be taken to ensure that appointees have enough time available to devote to the job. This is particularly important in the case of chairmanships.

The board should satisfy itself that plans are in place for orderly succession for appointments to the board and to senior management, so as to maintain an appropriate balance of skills and experience within the company and on the board.

Code Provisions

A.4.1   There should be a nomination committee which should lead the process for board appointments and make recommendations to the board. A majority of members of the nomination committee should be independent non-executive directors. The chairman or an independent non-executive director should chair the committee, but the chairman should not chair the nomination committee when it is dealing with the appointment of a successor to the chairmanship. The nomination committee should make available[8] its terms of reference, explaining its role and the authority delegated to it by the board.

A.4.2   The nomination committee should evaluate the balance of skills, knowledge and experience on the board and, in the light of this evaluation, prepare a description of the role and capabilities required for a particular appointment.

A.4.3   For the appointment of a chairman, the nomination committee should prepare a job specification, including an assessment of the time commitment expected, recognising the need for availability in the event of crises. A chairman's other significant commitments should be disclosed to the board before appointment and included in the annual report. Changes to such commitments should be reported to the board as they arise, and included in the next annual report. No individual should be appointed to a second chairmanship of a FTSE 100 company[9].

A.4.4   The terms and conditions of appointment of non-executive directors should be made available for inspection[10]. The letter of appointment should set out the expected time commitment. Non-executive directors should undertake that they will have sufficient time to meet what is expected of them. Their other significant commitments should be disclosed to the board before appointment, with a broad indication of the time involved and the board should be informed of subsequent changes.

A.4.5   The board should not agree to a full-time executive director taking on more than one non-executive directorship in a FTSE 100 company nor the chairmanship of such a company.

A.4.6   A separate section of the annual report should describe the work of the nomination committee, including the process it has used in relation to board appointments. An explanation should be given if neither an external search consultancy nor open advertising has been used in the appointment of a chairman or a non-executive director.

A.5 Information and professional development

Main Principle

The board should be supplied in a timely manner with information in a form and of a quality appropriate to enable it to discharge its duties. All directors should receive induction on joining the board and should regularly update and refresh their skills and knowledge.

Supporting Principles

The chairman is responsible for ensuring that the directors receive accurate, timely and clear information. Management has an obligation to provide such information but directors should seek clarification or amplification where necessary.

The chairman should ensure that the directors continually update their skills and the knowledge and familiarity with the company required to fulfil their role both on the board and on board committees. The company should provide the necessary resources for developing and updating its directors' knowledge and capabilities.

Under the direction of the chairman, the company secretary's responsibilities include ensuring good information flows within the board and its committees and between senior management and non-executive directors, as well as facilitating induction and assisting with professional development as required.

The company secretary should be responsible for advising the board through the chairman on all governance matters.

Code Provisions

A.5.1   The chairman should ensure that new directors receive a full, formal and tailored induction on joining the board. As part of this, the company should offer to major shareholders the opportunity to meet a new non-executive director.

A.5.2   The board should ensure that directors, especially non-executive directors, have access to independent professional advice at the company's expense where they judge it necessary to discharge their responsibilities as directors. Committees should be provided with sufficient resources to undertake their duties.

A.5.3   All directors should have access to the advice and services of the company secretary, who is responsible to the board for ensuring that board procedures are complied with. Both the appointment and removal of the company secretary should be a matter for the board as a whole.

A.6 Performance evaluation

Main Principle

The board should undertake a formal and rigorous annual evaluation of its own performance and that of its committees and individual directors.

Supporting Principle

Individual evaluation should aim to show whether each director continues to contribute effectively and to demonstrate commitment to the role (including commitment of time for board and committee meetings and any other duties). The chairman should act on the results of the performance evaluation by recognising the strengths and addressing the weaknesses of the board and, where appropriate, proposing new members be appointed to the board or seeking the resignation of directors.

Code Provision

A.6.1 The board should state in the annual report how performance evaluation of the board, its committees and its individual directors has been conducted. The non-executive directors, led by the senior independent director, should be responsible for performance evaluation of the chairman, taking into account the views of executive directors.

A.7 Re-election

Main Principle

All directors should be submitted for re-election at regular intervals, subject to continued satisfactory performance. The board should ensure planned and progressive refreshing of the board.

Code Provisions

A.7.1 All directors should be subject to election by shareholders at the first annual general meeting after their appointment, and to re-election thereafter at intervals of no more than three years. The names of directors submitted for election or re-election should be accompanied by sufficient biographical details and any other relevant information to enable shareholders to take an informed decision on their election.

A.7.2 Non-executive directors should be appointed for specified terms subject to re-election and to Companies Acts provisions relating to the removal of a director. The board should set out to shareholders in the papers accompanying a resolution to elect a non-executive director why they believe an individual should be elected. The chairman should confirm to shareholders when proposing re-election that, following formal performance evaluation, the individual's performance continues to be effective and to demonstrate commitment to the role. Any term beyond six years (e.g. two three-year terms) for a non-executive director should be subject to particularly rigorous review, and should take into account the need for progressive refreshing of the board. Non-executive directors may serve longer than nine years (e.g. three three-year terms), subject to annual re-election. Serving more than nine years could be relevant to the determination of a non-executive director's independence (as set out in provision A.3.1).

B. Remuneration

B.1 The Level and Make-up of Remuneration[11]

Main Principles

Levels of remuneration should be sufficient to attract, retain and motivate directors of the quality required to run the company successfully, but a company should avoid paying more than is necessary for this purpose. A significant proportion of executive directors' remuneration should be structured so as to link rewards to corporate and individual performance.

Supporting Principle

The remuneration committee should judge where to position their company relative to other companies. But they should use such comparisons with caution, in view of the risk of an upward ratchet of remuneration levels with no corresponding improvement in performance. They should also be sensitive to pay and employment conditions elsewhere in the group, especially when determining annual salary increases.

Code Provisions

Remuneration policy

B.1.1 The performance-related elements of remuneration should form a significant proportion of the total remuneration package of executive directors and should be designed to align their interests with those of shareholders and to give these directors keen incentives to perform at the highest levels. In designing schemes of performance-related remuneration, the remuneration committee should follow the provisions in Schedule A to this Code.

B.1.2 Executive share options should not be offered at a discount save as permitted by the relevant provisions of the Listing Rules.

B.1.3 Levels of remuneration for non-executive directors should reflect the time commitment and responsibilities of the role. Remuneration for non-executive directors should not include share options. If, exceptionally, options are granted, shareholder approval should be sought in advance and any shares acquired by exercise of the options should be held until at least one year after the non-executive director leaves the board. Holding of share options could be relevant to the determination of a non-executive director's independence (as set out in provision A.3.1).

B.1.4 Where a company releases an executive director to serve as a non-executive director elsewhere, the remuneration report[12] should include a statement as to whether or not the director will retain such earnings and, if so, what the remuneration is.

Service Contracts and Compensation

B.1.5 The remuneration committee should carefully consider what compensation commitments (including pension contributions and all other elements) their directors' terms of appointment would entail in the event of early termination. The aim should be to avoid rewarding poor performance. They should take a robust line on reducing compensation to reflect departing directors' obligations to mitigate loss.

B.1.6 Notice or contract periods should be set at one year or less. If it is necessary to offer longer notice or contract periods to new directors recruited from outside, such periods should reduce to one year or less after the initial period.

B.2 Procedure

Main Principle

There should be a formal and transparent procedure for developing policy on executive remuneration and for fixing the remuneration packages of individual directors. No director should be involved in deciding his or her own remuneration.

Supporting Principles

The remuneration committee should consult the chairman and/or chief executive about their proposals relating to the remuneration of other executive directors. The remuneration committee should also be responsible for appointing any consultants in respect of executive director remuneration. Where executive directors or senior management are involved in advising or supporting the remuneration committee, care should be taken to recognise and avoid conflicts of interest. The chairman of the board should ensure that the company maintains contact as required with its principal shareholders about remuneration in the same way as for other matters. .

Code Provisions

B.2.1 The board should establish a remuneration committee of at least three, or in the case of smaller companies[13] two, members, who should all be independent non-executive directors. The remuneration committee should make available[14] its terms of reference, explaining its role and the authority delegated to it by the board. Where remuneration consultants are appointed, a statement should be made available[15] of whether they have any other connection with the company.

B.2.2 The remuneration committee should have delegated responsibility for setting remuneration for all executive directors and the chairman, including pension rights and any compensation payments. The committee should also recommend and monitor the level and structure of remuneration for senior management. The definition of 'senior management' for this purpose should be determined by the board but should normally include the first layer of management below board level.

B.2.3 The board itself or, where required by the Articles of Association, the shareholders should determine the remuneration of the non-executive directors within the limits set in the Articles of Association. Where permitted by the Articles, the board may however delegate this responsibility to a committee, which might include the chief executive.

B.2.4   Shareholders should be invited specifically to approve all new long-term incentive schemes (as defined in the Listing Rules) and significant changes to existing schemes, save in the circumstances permitted by the Listing Rules.

C. Accountability and audit

C.1 Financial Reporting

Main Principle

The board should present a balanced and understandable assessment of the company's position and prospects.

Supporting Principle

The board's responsibility to present a balanced and understandable assessment extends to interim and other price-sensitive public reports and reports to regulators as well as to information required to be presented by statutory requirements.

Code Provisions

C.1.1   The directors should explain in the annual report their responsibility for preparing the accounts and there should be a statement by the auditors about their reporting responsibilities.

C.1.2   The directors should report that the business is a going concern, with supporting assumptions or qualifications as necessary.

C.2 Internal Control[16]

Main Principle

The board should maintain a sound system of internal control to safeguard shareholders' investment and the company's assets.

Code Provision

C.2.1   The board should, at least annually, conduct a review of the effectiveness of the group's system of internal controls and should report to shareholders that they have done so. The review should cover all material controls, including financial, operational and compliance controls and risk management systems.

C.3 Audit Committee and Auditors[17]

Main Principle

The board should establish formal and transparent arrangements for considering how they should apply the financial reporting and internal control principles and for maintaining an appropriate relationship with the company's auditors.

Code Provisions

C.3.1   The board should establish an audit committee of at least three, or in the case of smaller companies[18] two, members, who should all be independent non-executive directors. The board should satisfy itself that at least one member of the audit committee has recent and relevant financial experience.

C.3.2   The main role and responsibilities of the audit committee should be set out in written terms of reference and should include:
   • to monitor the integrity of the financial statements of the company, and any formal announcements relating to the company's financial performance, reviewing significant financial reporting judgements contained in them;
   • to review the company's internal financial controls and, unless expressly addressed by a separate board risk committee composed of independent directors, or by the board itself, to review the company's internal control and risk management systems;
   • to monitor and review the effectiveness of the company's internal audit function;
   • to make recommendations to the board, for it to put to the shareholders for their approval in general meeting, in relation to the appointment, re-appointment and removal of the external auditor and to approve the remuneration and terms of engagement of the external auditor;
   • to review and monitor the external auditor's independence and objectivity and the effectiveness of the audit process, taking into consideration relevant UK professional and regulatory requirements; and
   • to develop and implement policy on the engagement of the external auditor to supply non-audit services, taking into account relevant ethical guidance regarding the provision of non-audit services by the external audit firm; and to report to the board, identifying any matters in respect of which it considers that action or improvement is needed and making recommendations as to the steps to be taken.

C.3.3   The terms of reference of the audit committee, including its role and the authority delegated to it by the board, should be made available.[19] A separate section of the annual report should describe the work of the committee in discharging those responsibilities.

C.3.4   The audit committee should review arrangements by which staff of the company may, in confidence, raise concerns about possible improprieties in matters of financial reporting or other matters. The audit committee's objective should be to ensure that arrangements are in place for the proportionate and independent investigation of such matters and for appropriate follow-up action.

C.3.5   The audit committee should monitor and review the effectiveness of the internal audit activities. Where there is no internal audit function, the audit committee should consider annually whether there is a need for an internal audit function and make a recommendation to the board, and the reasons for the absence of such a function should be explained in the relevant section of the annual report.

C.3.6   The audit committee should have primary responsibility for making a recommendation on the appointment, reappointment and removal of the external auditors. If the board does not accept the audit committee's recommendation, it should include in the annual report, and in any papers recommending appointment or re-appointment, a statement from the audit committee explaining the recommendation and should set out reasons why the board has taken a different position.

C.3.7   The annual report should explain to shareholders how, if the auditor provides non-audit services, auditor objectivity and independence is safeguarded.

D. Relations with shareholders

D.1 Dialogue with Institutional Shareholders

Main Principle

There should be a dialogue with shareholders based on the mutual understanding of objectives. The board as a whole has responsibility for ensuring that a satisfactory dialogue with shareholders takes place.[20]

Supporting Principles

Whilst recognising that most shareholder contact is with the chief executive and finance director, the chairman (and the senior independent director and other directors as appropriate) should maintain sufficient contact with major shareholders to understand their issues and concerns. The board should keep in touch with shareholder opinion in whatever ways are most practical and efficient.

Code Provisions

D.1.1   The chairman should ensure that the views of shareholders are communicated to the board as a whole. The chairman should discuss governance and strategy with major shareholders. Non-executive directors should be offered the opportunity to attend meetings with major shareholders and should expect to attend them if requested by major shareholders. The senior independent director should attend sufficient meetings with a range of major shareholders to listen to their views in order to help develop a balanced understanding of the issues and concerns of major shareholders.

D.1.2   The board should state in the annual report the steps they have taken to ensure that the members of the board, and in particular the non-executive directors, develop an understanding of the views of major shareholders about their company, for example through direct face-to-face contact, analysts' or brokers' briefings and surveys of shareholder opinion.

D.2 Constructive Use of the AGM

Main Principle

The board should use the AGM to communicate with investors and to encourage their participation.

Code Provisions

D.2.1   The company should count all proxy votes and, except where a poll is called, should indicate the level of proxies lodged on each resolution, and the balance for and against the resolution and the number of abstentions, after it has been dealt with on a show of hands. The company should ensure that votes cast are properly received and recorded.

D.2.2   The company should propose a separate resolution at the AGM on each substantially separate issue and should in particular propose a resolution at the AGM relating to the report and accounts.

D.2.3   The chairman should arrange for the chairmen of the audit, remuneration and nomination committees to be available to answer questions at the AGM and for all directors to attend.

D.2.4   The company should arrange for the Notice of the AGM and related papers to be sent to shareholders at least 20 working days before the meeting.

Section 2 Institutional shareholders

E. Institutional shareholders [21]

E.1 Dialogue with companies

Main Principle

Institutional shareholders should enter into a dialogue with companies based on the mutual understanding of objectives.

Supporting Principles

Institutional shareholders should apply the principles set out in the Institutional Shareholders' Committee's 'The Responsibilities of Institutional Shareholders and Agents — Statement of Principles'[22], which should be reflected in fund manager contracts.

E.2 Evaluation of Governance Disclosures

Main Principle

When evaluating companies' governance arrangements, particularly those relating to board structure and composition, institutional shareholders should give due weight to all relevant factors drawn to their attention.

Supporting Principle

Institutional shareholders should consider carefully explanations given for departure from this Code and make reasoned judgements in each case. They should give an explanation to the company, in writing where appropriate, and be prepared to enter a dialogue if they do not accept the company's position. They should avoid a box-ticking approach to assessing a company's corporate governance. They should bear in mind in particular the size and complexity of the company and the nature of the risks and challenges it faces.

E.3 Shareholder Voting

Main Principle

Institutional shareholders have a responsibility to make considered use of their votes.

Supporting Principles

Institutional shareholders should take steps to ensure their voting intentions are being translated into practice.

Institutional shareholders should, on request, make available to their clients information on the proportion of resolutions on which votes were cast and non-discretionary proxies lodged.

Major shareholders should attend AGMs where appropriate and practicable. Companies and registrars should facilitate this.

Schedule A: Provisions on the design of performance related remuneration

1   The remuneration committee should consider whether the directors should be eligible for annual bonuses. If so, performance conditions should be relevant, stretching and designed to enhance shareholder value. Upper limits should be set and disclosed. There may be a case for part payment in shares to be held for a significant period.

2   The remuneration committee should consider whether the directors should be eligible for benefits under long-term incentive schemes. Traditional share option schemes should be weighed against other kinds of long-term incentive scheme. In normal circumstances, shares granted or other forms of deferred remuneration should not vest, and options should not be exercisable, in less than three years. Directors should be encouraged to hold their shares for a further period after vesting or exercise, subject to the need to finance any costs of acquisition and associated tax liabilities.

3   Any new long-term incentive schemes which are proposed should be approved by share-holders and should preferably replace any existing schemes or at least form part of a well considered overall plan, incorporating existing schemes. The total rewards potentially available should not be excessive.

4   Payouts or grants under all incentive schemes, including new grants under existing share option schemes, should be subject to challenging performance criteria reflecting the company's objectives. Consideration should be given to criteria which reflect the company's performance relative to a group of comparator companies in some key variables such as total shareholder return.

5   Grants under executive share option and other long-term incentive schemes should normally be phased rather than awarded in one large block.

6   In general, only basic salary should be pensionable.

7   The remuneration committee should consider the pension consequences and associated costs to the company of basic salary increases and any other changes in pensionable remuneration, especially for directors close to retirement.

Schedule B: Guidance on liability of non-executive directors: care, skill and diligence

1   Although non-executive directors and executive directors have as board members the same legal duties and objectives, the time devoted to the company's affairs is likely to be significantly less for a non-executive director than for an executive director and the detailed knowledge and experience of a company's affairs that could reasonably be expected of a non-executive director will generally be less than for an executive director. These matters may be relevant in assessing the knowledge, skill and experience which may reasonably be expected of a non-executive director and therefore the care, skill and diligence that a non-executive director may be expected to exercise.

2   In this context, the following elements of the Code may also be particularly relevant.

(i)   In order to enable directors to fulfil their duties, the Code states that:
- The letter of appointment of the director should set out the expected time commitment (Code provision A.4.4); and
- The board should be supplied in a timely manner with information in a form and of a quality appropriate to enable it to discharge its duties. The chairman is responsible for ensuring that the directors are provided by management with accurate, timely and clear information. (Code principles A.5)

(ii)   Non-executive directors should themselves:
- Undertake appropriate induction and regularly update and refresh their skills, knowledge and familiarity with the company (Code principle A.5 and provision A.5.1)
- Seek appropriate clarification or amplification of information and, where necessary, take and follow appropriate professional advice. (Code principle A.5 and provision A.5.2)

- Where they have concerns about the running of the company or a proposed action, ensure that these are addressed by the board and, to the extent that they are not resolved, ensure that they are recorded in the board minutes. (Code provision A.1.4)
- Give a statement to the board if they have such unresolved concerns on resignation. (Code provision A.1.4)

3   It is up to each non-executive director to reach a view as to what is necessary in particular circumstances to comply with the duty of care, skill and diligence they owe as a director to the company. In considering whether or not a person is in breach of that duty, a court would take into account all relevant circumstances. These may include having regard to the above where relevant to the issue of liability of a non-executive director.

Schedule C: Disclosure of corporate governance arrangements

The Listing Rules require a statement to be included in the annual report relating to compliance with the Code, as described in the preamble.

For ease of reference, the specific requirements in the Code for disclosure are set out below:

The annual report should record:

- a statement of how the board operates, including a high level statement of which types of decisions are to be taken by the board and which are to be delegated to management (A.1.1);
- the names of the chairman, the deputy chairman (where there is one), the chief executive, the senior independent director and the chairmen and members of the nomination, audit and remuneration committees (A.1.2);
- the number of meetings of the board and those committees and individual attendance by directors (A.1.2);
- the names of the non-executive directors whom the board determines to be independent, with reasons where necessary (A.3.1);
- the other significant commitments of the chairman and any changes to them during the year (A.4.3);
- how performance evaluation of the board, its committees and its directors has been conducted (A.6.1); and
- the steps the board has taken to ensure that members of the board, and in particular the non-executive directors, develop an understanding of the views of major shareholders about their company (D.1.2).

The report should also include:

- a separate section describing the work of the nomination committee, including the process it has used in relation to board appointments and an explanation if neither external search consultancy nor open advertising has been used in the appointment of a chairman or a non-executive director (A.4.6);
- a description of the work of the remuneration committee as required under the Directors' Remuneration Reporting Regulations 2002, and including, where an executive director

serves as a non-executive director elsewhere, whether or not the director will retain such earnings and, if so, what the remuneration is (B.1.4);

- an explanation from the directors of their responsibility for preparing the accounts and a statement by the auditors about their reporting responsibilities (C.1.1);
- a statement from the directors that the business is a going concern, with supporting assumptions or qualifications as necessary (C.1.2);
- a report that the board has conducted a review of the effectiveness of the group's system of internal controls (C.2.1);
- a separate section describing the work of the audit committee in discharging its responsibilities (C.3.3);
- where there is no internal audit function, the reasons for the absence of such a function (C.3.5);
- where the board does not accept the audit committee's recommendation on the appointment, reappointment or removal of an external auditor, a statement from the audit committee explaining the recommendation and the reasons why the board has taken a different position (C.3.6); and
- an explanation of how, if the auditor provides non-audit services, auditor objectivity and independence is safeguarded (C.3.7).

The following information should be made available (which may be met by making it available on request and placing the information available on the company's website):

- the terms of reference of the nomination, remuneration and audit committees, explaining their role and the authority delegated to them by the board (A.4.1, B.2.1 and C.3.3);
- the terms and conditions of appointment of non-executive directors (A.4.4) (see footnote 10); and
- where remuneration consultants are appointed, a statement of whether they have any other connection with the company (B.2.1).

The board should set out to shareholders in the papers accompanying a resolution to elect or re-elect:

- sufficient biographical details to enable shareholders to take an informed decision on their election or re-election (A.7.1);
- why they believe an individual should be elected to a non-executive role (A.7.2); and
- on re-election of a non-executive director, confirmation from the chairman that, following formal performance evaluation, the individual's performance continues to be effective and to demonstrate commitment to the role, including commitment of time for board and committee meetings and any other duties (A.7.2).

The board should set out to shareholders in the papers recommending appointment or re-appointment of an external auditor:

- if the board does not accept the audit committee's recommendation, a statement from the audit committee explaining the recommendation and from the board setting out reasons why they have taken a different position. (C.3.6).

Notes to the Combined Code

1   Review of the role and effectiveness of non-executive directors, published January 2003.

2   Audit Committees Combined Code Guidance, published January 2003.

3   Internal Control: Guidance for Directors on the Combined Code, published by the Institute of Chartered Accountants in England and Wales in September 1999.

4   The Directors' Remuneration Report Regulations 2002, SI no. 1986.

5   Compliance or otherwise with this provision need only be reported for the year in which the appointment is made.

6   A.2.2 states that the chairman should, on appointment, meet the independence criteria set out in this provision, but thereafter the test of independence is not appropriate in relation to the chairman.

7   A smaller company is one that is below the FTSE 350 throughout the year immediately prior to the reporting year.

8   The requirement to make the information available would be met by making it available on request and by including the information on the company's website.

9   Compliance or otherwise with this provision need only be reported for the year in which the appointment is made.

10 The terms and conditions of appointment of non-executive directors should be made available for inspection by any person at the company's registered office during normal business hours and at the AGM (for 15 minutes prior to the meeting and during the meeting).

11 Views have been sought by the Department of Trade and Industry by 30 September 2003 on whether, and, if so how, further measures are required to enable shareholders to ensure that compensation reflects performance when directors' contracts are terminated: See 'Rewards for Failure': Directors' Remuneration — Contracts, performance and severance, June 2003.

12 As required under the Directors' Remuneration Report Regulations.

13 See footnote 7.

14 See footnote 8.

15 See footnote 8.

16 The Turnbull Guidance suggests means of applying this part of the Code.

17 The Smith Guidance suggests means of applying this part of the Code.

18 See footnote 7.

19 See footnote 8.

20 Nothing in these principles or provisions should be taken to override the general requirements of law to treat shareholders equally in access to information.

21 Agents such as investment managers, or voting services, are frequently appointed by institutional shareholders to act on their behalf and these principles should accordingly be read as applying where appropriate to the agents of institutional shareholders.

22 Available at website: www.investmentuk.org.uk/press/2002/20021021-01.pdf.

Suggestions for good practice from the Higgs Report

Guidance on the role of the chairman

The chairman is pivotal in creating the conditions for overall board and individual director effectiveness, both inside and outside the boardroom. Specifically, it is the responsibility of the chairman to:

- run the board and set its agenda. The agenda should take full account of the issues and the concerns of all board members. Agendas should be forward looking and concentrate on strategic matters rather than formulaic approvals of proposals which can be the subject of appropriate delegated powers to management;
- ensure that the members of the board receive accurate, timely and clear information, in particular about the company's performance, to enable the board to take sound decisions, monitor effectively and provide advice to promote the success of the company;
- ensure effective communication with shareholders and ensure that the members of the board develop an understanding of the views of the major investors;
- manage the board to ensure that sufficient time is allowed for discussion of complex or contentious issues, where appropriate arranging for informal meetings beforehand to enable thorough preparation for the board discussion. It is particularly important that non-executive directors have sufficient time to consider critical issues and are not faced with unrealistic deadlines for decision-making;
- take the lead in providing a properly constructed induction programme for new directors that is comprehensive, formal and tailored, facilitated by the company secretary;
- take the lead in identifying and meeting the development needs of individual directors, with the company secretary having a key role in facilitating provision. It is the responsibility of the chairman to address the development needs of the board as a whole with a view to enhancing its overall effectiveness as a team;
- ensure that the performance of individuals and of the board as a whole and its committees is evaluated at least once a year; and
- encourage active engagement by all the members of the board.

The effective chairman:

- upholds the highest standards of integrity and probity;
- sets the agenda, style and tone of board discussions to promote effective decision-making and constructive debate;
- promotes effective relationships and open communication, both inside and outside the boardroom, between non-executive directors and executive team;
- builds an effective and complementary board, initiating change and planning succession in board appointments, subject to board and shareholders' approval;
- promotes the highest standards of corporate governance and seeks compliance with the provisions of the Code wherever possible;
- ensures clear structure for and the effective running of board committees;
- ensures effective implementation of board decisions;

- establishes a close relationship of trust with the chief executive, providing support and advice while respecting executive responsibility; and
- provides coherent leadership of the company, including representing the company and understanding the views of shareholders.

Guidance on the role of the non-executive director

As members of the unitary board, all directors are required to:

- provide entrepreneurial leadership of the company within a framework of prudent and effective controls which enable risk to be assessed and managed;
- set the company's strategic aims, ensure that the necessary financial and human resources are in place for the company to meet its objectives, and review management performance; and
- set the company's values and standards and ensure that its obligations to its shareholders and others are understood and met.

In addition to these requirements for all directors, the role of the non-executive director has the following key elements:

- Strategy. Non-executive directors should constructively challenge and help develop proposals on strategy.
- Performance. Non-executive directors should scrutinise the performance of management in meeting agreed goals and objectives and monitor the reporting of performance.
- Risk. Non-executive directors should satisfy themselves on the integrity of financial information and that financial controls and systems of risk management are robust and defensible.
- People. Non-executive directors are responsible for determining appropriate levels of remuneration of executive directors, and have a prime role in appointing, and where necessary removing, executive directors and in succession planning.

Non-executive directors should constantly seek to establish and maintain confidence in the conduct of the company. They should be independent in judgement and have an enquiring mind. To be effective, non-executive directors need to build a recognition by executives of their contribution in order to promote openness and trust.

To be effective, non-executive directors need to be well-informed about the company and the external environment in which it operates, with a strong command of issues relevant to the business. A non-executive director should insist on a comprehensive, formal and tailored induction. An effective induction need not be restricted to the boardroom, so consideration should be given to visiting sites and meeting senior and middle management. Once in post, an effective non-executive director should seek continually to develop and refresh their knowledge and skills to ensure that their contribution to the board remains informed and relevant.

Best practice dictates that an effective non-executive director will ensure that information is provided sufficiently in advance of meetings to enable thorough consideration of the issues facing the board. The non-executive should insist that information is sufficient, accurate, clear and timely.

An element of the role of the non-executive director is to understand the views of major investors both directly and through the chairman and the senior independent director.

The effective non-executive director:

- upholds the highest ethical standards of integrity and probity;
- supports executives in their leadership of the business while monitoring their conduct;
- questions intelligently, debates constructively, challenges rigorously and decides dispassionately;
- listens sensitively to the views of others, inside and outside the board;
- gains the trust and respect of other board members; and
- promotes the highest standards of corporate governance and seeks compliance with the provisions of the Code wherever possible.

Summary of the principal duties of the remuneration committee

The Code provides that the remuneration committee should consist exclusively of independent non-executive directors and should comprise at least three or, in the case of smaller companies, two such directors.

Duties

The committee should:

- determine and agree with the board the framework or broad policy for the remuneration of the chief executive, the chairman of the company and such other members of the executive management as it is designated to consider. As a minimum, the committee should have delegated responsibility for setting remuneration for all executive directors, the chairman and, to maintain and assure their independence, the company secretary. The remuneration of non-executive directors shall be a matter for the chairman and executive members of the board. No director or manager should be involved in any decisions as to their own remuneration;
- determine targets for any performance-related pay schemes operated by the company;
- determine the policy for and scope of pension arrangements for each executive director;
- ensure that contractual terms on termination, and any payments made, are fair to the individual and the company, that failure is not rewarded and that the duty to mitigate loss is fully recognised;
- within the terms of the agreed policy, determine the total individual remuneration package of each executive director including, where appropriate, bonuses, incentive payments and share options;

- in determining such packages and arrangements, give due regard to the contents of the Code as well as the UK Listing Authority's Listing Rules and associated guidance;
- be aware of and advise on any major changes in employee benefit structures throughout the company or group;
- agree the policy for authorising claims for expenses from the chief executive and chairman;
- ensure that provisions regarding disclosure of remuneration, including pensions, as set out in the Directors' Remuneration Report Regulations 2002 and the Code, are fulfilled;
- be exclusively responsible for establishing the selection criteria, selecting, appointing and setting the terms of reference for any remuneration consultants who advise the committee;
- report the frequency of, and attendance by members at, remuneration committee meetings in the annual reports; and
- make available the committee's terms of reference. These should set out the committee's delegated responsibilities and be reviewed and, where necessary, updated annually.

This guidance has been compiled with the assistance of ICSA who have kindly agreed to produce updated guidance on their website www.icsa.org.uk in the future.

Notes:
1 A smaller company is one that is below the FTSE 350 throughout the year immediately prior to the reporting year.
2 Some companies require the remuneration committee to consider the packages of all executives at or above a specified level such as those reporting to a main board director whilst others require the committee to deal with all packages above a certain figure.
3 Remuneration committees should consider reviewing and agreeing a standard form of contract for their executive directors, and ensuring that new appointees are offered and accept terms within the previously agreed level.

Summary of the principal duties of the nomination committee

There should be a nomination committee which should lead the process for board appointments and make recommendations to the board.

A majority of members of the committee should be independent non-executive directors. The chairman or an independent non-executive director should chair the committee, but the chairman should not chair the nomination committee when it is dealing with the appointment of a successor to the chairmanship.

Duties

The committee should:

- be responsible for identifying and nominating for the approval of the board, candidates to fill board vacancies as and when they arise;

- before making an appointment, evaluate the balance of skills, knowledge and experience on the board and, in the light of this evaluation, prepare a description of the role and capabilities required for a particular appointment;
- review annually the time required from a non-executive director. Performance evaluation should be used to assess whether the non-executive director is spending enough time to fulfil their duties;
- consider candidates from a wide range of backgrounds and look beyond the 'usual suspects';
- give full consideration to succession planning in the course of its work, taking into account the challenges and opportunities facing the company and what skills and expertise are therefore needed on the board in the future;
- regularly review the structure, size and composition (including the skills, knowledge and experience) of the board and make recommendations to the board with regard to any changes;
- keep under review the leadership needs of the organisation, both executive and non-executive, with a view to ensuring the continued ability of the organisation to compete effectively in the marketplace;
- make a statement in the annual report about its activities; the process used for appointments and explain if external advice or open advertising has not been used; the membership of the committee, number of committee meetings and attendance over the course of the year;
- make available its terms of reference explaining clearly its role and the authority delegated to it by the board; and
- ensure that on appointment to the board, non-executive directors receive a formal letter of appointment setting out clearly what is expected of them in terms of time commitment, committee service and involvement outside board meetings.

The committee should make recommendations to the board:

- as regards plans for succession for both executive and non-executive directors;
- as regards the re-appointment of any non-executive director at the conclusion of their specified term of office;
- concerning the re-election by shareholders of any director under the retirement by rotation provisions in the company's articles of association;
- concerning any matters relating to the continuation in office of any director at any time; and
- concerning the appointment of any director to executive or other office other than to the positions of chairman and chief executive, the recommendation for which would be considered at a meeting of the board.

This guidance has been compiled with the assistance of ICSA who have kindly agreed to produce updated guidance on their website www.icsa.org.uk in the future.

Pre-appointment due diligence checklist for new board members

Why?

Before accepting an appointment a prospective non-executive director should undertake their own thorough examination of the company to satisfy themselves that it is an organisation in which they can have faith and in which they will be well suited to working.

The following questions are not intended to be exhaustive, but are intended to be a helpful basis of the pre-appointment due diligence process that all non-executive directors should undertake.

Questions to ask

What is the company's current financial position and what has its financial track record been over the last three years?

What are the key dependencies (e.g. regulatory approvals, key licences, etc)?

What record does the company have on corporate governance issues?

If the company is not performing particularly well is there potential to turn it round and do I have the time, desire and capability to make a positive impact?

What is the exact nature and extent of the company's business activities?

Who are the current executive and non-executive directors, what is their background and their record and how long have they served on the board?

What is the size and structure of the board and board committees and what are the relationships between the chairman and the board, the chief executive and the management team?

Who owns the company i.e. who are the company's main shareholders and how has the profile changed over recent years? What is the company's attitude towards, and relationship with, its shareholders?

Is any material litigation presently being undertaken or threatened, either by the company or against it?

Is the company clear and specific about the qualities, knowledge, skills and experience that it needs to complement the existing board?

What insurance cover is available to directors and what is the company's policy on indemnifying directors?

Do I have the necessary knowledge, skills, experience and time to make a positive contribution to the board of this company?

How closely do I match the job specification and how well will I fulfil the board's expectations?

Is there anything about the nature and extent of the company's business activities that would cause me concern both in terms of risk and any personal ethical considerations?

Am I satisfied that the internal regulation of the company is sound and that I can operate effectively within its stated corporate governance framework?

Am I satisfied that the size, structure and make-up of the board will enable me to make an effective contribution?

Would accepting the non-executive directorship put me in a position of having a conflict of interest?

Sources of information

- Company report and accounts, and/or any listing prospectus, for the recent years;
- Analyst reports;
- Press reports;
- Company website;
- Any Corporate Social Responsibility or Environmental Report issued by the company;
- Rating agency reports; and
- Voting services reports.

Published material is unlikely to reveal wrong-doing. However, a lack of transparency may be a reason to proceed with caution.

This guidance has been compiled with the assistance of ICSA who have kindly agreed to produce updated guidance on their website www.icsa.org.uk in the future.

Sample letter of non-executive director appointment

On [date], upon the recommendation of the nomination committee, the board of [company] ('the Company') has appointed you as non-executive director. I am writing to set out the terms of your appointment. It is agreed that this is a contract for services and is not a contract of employment.

Appointment

Your appointment will be for an initial term of three years commencing on [date], unless otherwise terminated earlier by and at the discretion of either party upon [one month's] written notice. Continuation of your contract of appointment is contingent on satisfactory performance and re-election at forthcoming AGMs. Non-executive directors are typically expected to serve two three-year terms, although the board may invite you to serve an additional period.

Time commitment

Overall we anticipate a time commitment of [number] days per month after the induction phase. This will include attendance at [monthly] board meetings, the AGM, [one] annual board away day, and [at least one] site visit per year. In addition, you will be expected to devote appropriate preparation time ahead of each meeting.

By accepting this appointment, you have confirmed that you are able to allocate sufficient time to meet the expectations of your role. The agreement of the chairman should be sought before accepting additional commitments that might impact on the time you are able to devote to your role as a non-executive director of the company.

Role

Non-executive directors have the same general legal responsibilities to the company as any other director. The board as a whole is collectively responsible for the success of the company. The board:

- provides entrepreneurial leadership of the company within a framework of prudent and effective controls which enable risk to be assessed and managed;
- sets the company's strategic aims, ensures that the necessary financial and human resources are in place for the company to meet its objectives, and reviews management performance; and
- sets the company's values and standards and ensure that its obligations to its shareholders and others are understood and met.

All directors must take decisions objectively in the interests of the company.

In addition to these requirements of all directors, the role of the non-executive director has the following key elements:

- Strategy. Non-executive directors should constructively challenge and help develop proposals on strategy;
- Performance. Non-executive directors should scrutinise the performance of management in meeting agreed goals and objectives and monitor the reporting of performance;
- Risk. Non-executive directors should satisfy themselves on the integrity of financial information and that financial controls and systems of risk management are robust and defensible; and
- People. Non-executive directors are responsible for determining appropriate levels of remuneration of executive directors and have a prime role in appointing, and where necessary removing, executive directors and in succession planning.

Fees

You will be paid a fee of £[amount] gross per annum which will be paid monthly in arrears, [plus [number] ordinary shares of the company per annum, both of] which will be subject to an annual review by the board. The company will reimburse you for all reasonable and properly documented expenses you incur in performing the duties of your office.

Outside interests

It is accepted and acknowledged that you have business interests other than those of the company and have declared any conflicts that are apparent at present. In the event that you become aware of any potential conflicts of interest, these should be disclosed to the chairman and company secretary as soon as apparent.

[The board of the Company have determined you to be independent according to provision A.3.1 of the Code.]

Confidentiality

All information acquired during your appointment is confidential to the Company and should not be released, either during your appointment or following termination (by whatever means), to third parties without prior clearance from the chairman.

Your attention is also drawn to the requirements under both legislation and regulation as to the disclosure of price sensitive information. Consequently you should avoid making any statements that might risk a breach of these requirements without prior clearance from the chairman or company secretary.

Induction

Immediately after appointment, the Company will provide a comprehensive, formal and tailored induction. This will include the information pack recommended by the Institute of Chartered Secretaries and Administrators (ICSA), available at www.icsa.org.uk. We will also arrange for site visits and meetings with senior and middle management and the Company's auditors. We will also offer to major shareholders the opportunity to meet you.

Review process

The performance of individual directors and the whole board and its committees is evaluated annually. If, in the interim, there are any matters which cause you concern about your role you should discuss them with the chairman as soon as is appropriate.

Insurance

The Company has directors' and officers' liability insurance and it is intended to maintain such cover for the full term of your appointment. The current indemnity limit is £ [amount]; a copy of the policy document is attached.

Independent professional advice

Occasions may arise when you consider that you need professional advice in the furtherance of your duties as a director. Circumstances may occur when it will be appropriate for you to seek advice from independent advisors at the company's expense. A copy of the board's agreed procedure under which directors may obtain such independent advice is attached. The Company will reimburse the full cost of expenditure incurred in accordance with the attached policy.

Committees

This letter refers to your appointment as a non-executive director of the Company. In the event that you are also asked to serve on one or more of the board committees this will be covered in a separate communication setting out the committee(s)'s terms of reference, any specific responsibilities and any additional fees that may be involved.

This sample appointment letter has been complied with the assistance of ICSA who have kindly agreed to produce updated guidance on their website www.icsa.org.uk in the future.

Induction checklist

Guidance on Induction

Every company should develop its own comprehensive, formal induction programme that is tailored to the needs of the company and individual non-executive directors. The following guidelines might form the core of an induction programme.

As a general rule, a combination of selected written information together with presentations and activities such as meetings and site visits will help to give a new appointee a balanced and real-life overview of the company. Care should be taken not to overload the new director with too much information. The new non-executive director should be provided with a list of all the induction information that is being made available to them so that they may call up items if required before otherwise provided.

The induction process should:

1. Build an understanding of the nature of the company, its business and the markets in which it operates. For example, induction should cover:
   - the company's products or services;
   - group structure/subsidiaries/joint ventures;
   - the company's constitution, board procedures and matters reserved for the board;
   - summary details of the company's principal assets, liabilities, significant contracts and major competitors;
   - the company's major risks and risk management strategy;
   - key performance indicators; and
   - regulatory constraints.

2. Build a link with the company's people, including;
   - meetings with senior management;
   - visits to company sites other than the headquarters, to learn about production or services and meet employees in an informal setting. It is important, not only for the board to get to know the new non-executive director, but also for the non-executive director to build a profile with employees below board level; and
   - participating in board strategy development. 'Awaydays' enable a new non-executive director to begin to build working relationships away from the formal setting of the boardroom.

3. Build an understanding of the company's main relationships including meeting with the auditors and developing a knowledge of in particular:
   - who are the major customers;
   - who are the major suppliers;
   - who are the major shareholders and what is the shareholder relations policy; and

- participation in meetings with shareholders can help give a first hand feel as well as letting shareholders know who the non-executive directors are.

The induction pack

On appointment, or during the weeks immediately following, a new non-executive director should be provided with certain basic information to help ensure their early effective contribution to the company. ICSA has produced, and undertaken to maintain, on its website www.icsa.org a guidance note detailing a full list of such material.

Performance evaluation guidance

Guidance on performance evaluation

The Code provides that the board should undertake a formal and rigorous annual evaluation of its own performance and that of its committees and individual directors. Individual evaluation should aim to show whether each director continues to contribute effectively and to demonstrate commitment to the role (including commitment of time for board and committee meetings and any other duties). The chairman should act on the results of the performance evaluation by recognising the strengths and addressing the weaknesses of the board and, where appropriate, proposing new members be appointed to the board or seeking the resignation of directors. The board should state in the annual report how such performance evaluation has been conducted.

It is the responsibility of the chairman to select an effective process and to act on its outcome. The use of an external third party to conduct the evaluation will bring objectivity to the process.

The non-executive directors, led by the senior independent director, should be responsible for performance evaluation of the chairman, taking into account the views of executive directors.

The evaluation process will be used constructively as a mechanism to improve board effectiveness, maximise strengths and tackle weaknesses. The results of board evaluation should be shared with the board as a whole while the results of individual assessments should remain confidential between the chairman and the non-executive director concerned.

The following are some of the questions that should be considered in a performance evaluation. They are, however, by no means definitive or exhaustive and companies will wish to tailor the questions to suit their own needs and circumstances.

The responses to these questions and others should enable boards to assess how they are performing and to identify how certain elements of their performance areas might be improved.

Performance evaluation of the board

- How well has the board performed against any performance objectives that have been set?
- What has been the board's contribution to the testing and development of strategy?
- What has been the board's contribution to ensuring robust and effective risk management?

- Is the composition of the board and its committees appropriate, with the right mix of knowledge and skills to maximise performance in the light of future strategy? Are inside and outside the board relationships working effectively?
- How has the board responded to any problems or crises that have emerged and could or should these have been foreseen?
- Are the matters specifically reserved for the board the right ones?
- How well does the board communicate with the management team, company employees and others? How effectively does it use mechanisms such as the AGM and the annual report?
- Is the board as a whole up to date with latest developments in the regulatory environment and the market?
- How effective are the board's committees? [Specific questions on the performance of each committee should be included such as, for example, their role, their composition and their interaction with the board.]

The processes that help underpin the board's effectiveness should also be evaluated e.g.:

- Is appropriate, timely information of the right length and quality provided to the board and is management responsive to requests for clarification or amplification? Does the board provide helpful feedback to management on its requirements?
- Are sufficient board and committee meetings of appropriate length held to enable proper consideration of issues? Is time used effectively?
- Are board procedures conducive to effective performance and flexible enough to deal with all eventualities?

In addition, there are some specific issues relating to the chairman which should be included as part of an evaluation of the board's performance e.g.:

- Is the chairman demonstrating effective leadership of the board?
- Are relationships and communications with shareholders well managed?
- Are relationships and communications within the board constructive?
- Are the processes for setting the agenda working? Do they enable board members to raise issues and concerns?
- Is the company secretary being used appropriately and to maximum value?

Performance evaluation of the non-executive director

The chairman and other board members should consider the following issues and the individual concerned should also be asked to assess themselves. For each non-executive director:

- How well prepared and informed are they for board meetings and is their meeting attendance satisfactory?
- Do they demonstrate a willingness to devote time and effort to understand the company and its business and a readiness to participate in events outside the boardroom such as site visits?
- What has been the quality and value of their contributions at board meetings?
- What has been their contribution to development of strategy and to risk management?

- How successfully have they brought their knowledge and experience to bear in the consideration of strategy?
- How effectively have they probed to test information and assumptions? Where necessary, how resolute are they in maintaining their own views and resisting pressure from others?
- How effectively and proactively have they followed up their areas of concern?
- How effective and successful are their relationships with fellow board members, the company secretary and senior management? Does their performance and behaviour engender mutual trust and respect within the board?
- How actively and successfully do they refresh their knowledge and skills and are they up to date with:
  - the latest developments in areas such as corporate governance framework and financial reporting ; and
  - the industry and market conditions?
- How well do they communicate with fellow board members, senior management and others, for example shareholders? Are they able to present their views convincingly yet diplomatically and do they listen and take on board the views of others?

Index